PRODUCING THE MUSICAL

PRODUCING THE MUSICAL

A GUIDE FOR SCHOOL,
COLLEGE, AND
COMMUNITY THEATRES

HALLER LAUGHLIN
AND
RANDY WHEELER

GREENWOOD PRESS
WESTPORT, CONNECTICUT • LONDON, ENGLAND

Library of Congress Cataloging in Publication Data

Laughlin, Haller.
  Producing the musical.

  Bibliography: p.
  Includes index.
  1. Musical revue, comedy, etc.—Production and
direction. I. Wheeler, Randy. II. Title.
MT955.L38   1984   782.81'07   83-22704
ISBN 0-313-24100-7 (lib. bdg.)

Library of Congress Catalog Card Number: 83-22704
ISBN: 0-313-24100-7

First published in 1984

Greenwood Press
A division of Congressional Information Service, Inc.
88 Post Road West, Westport, Connecticut 06881

Printed in the United States of America

10 9 8 7 6 5 4 3 2 1

To Jacque, my favorite star,
from Randy

To Mildred Farrey and Margaret Gerber,
who know the secret of "perfect harmony,"
from Haller

CONTENTS

ILLUSTRATIONS

PREFACE

Broadway started producing musical comedies (then called operettas) well before the turn of the twentieth century. Hollywood, even before the advent of sound, used musical comedy scripts as the bases for movies, with movie house pianos tinkling the melodies that audiences already recognized. Amateur theatres, however, were very late to produce musicals, no matter how great the audience demand. During the first half of the twentieth century, high schools endlessly trotted out yearly renditions from Gilbert and Sullivan's repertoire. The more sophisticated colleges occasionally tried an original musical or revue, with some institutions daring to attempt Rudolph Friml operettas or, perhaps, Franz Lehar's *The Merry Widow*. Community theatres rarely ventured beyond an imitation vaudeville or minstrel show.

With the advent of the 1960s, however, amateur producers began to realize that, no matter how inadequately they might be produced, musicals could be big money-makers, whether the producer was a high school teacher, a community theatre director, or a resident theatre manager. For one of the present authors the realization that even high schools were leaping into the Broadway musical market occurred in the mid-1960s with an invitation to see a nearby high school production of *Camelot*. The musical, produced at a three-session county high school, had a cast of 170 and a different chorus for each scene. The choruses from the preceding and succeeding scenes stood in the wings and sang the chorus numbers offstage along with their onstage counterparts. One shudders to think how close directing that production must have been to directing traffic and how chilly the backstage singers must have been standing there in their underwear, while those onstage wore the costumes. Nonetheless, the audiences loved it, and it played for eight sold-out performances, undoubtedly making a fortune for the school.

Just recently a designer friend visited her hometown and stopped by her old high school where *Bells Are Ringing* was rehearsing. The director announced that they were in their second month of rehearsals, with a month to go. When the designer remarked that they were certainly spending a great deal of time on the production, the director replied, "Oh, yes. They're going to be perfect! Why, you can hardly tell even now that they're pantomiming to records!"

This book is for people who direct musicals in which they do not expect a young high school girl in Virginia to open her mouth and have Judy Holliday's voice come out. High school, college, and resident theatre musicals can be produced without a lot of fuss, without a lot of expense, but with a great deal of taste.

There are numerous reasons for producing a musical instead of a nonmusical. Musicals are universally successful and can bolster a flagging season financially in a way that no other type of production can. They offer a tremendous opportunity for high school, college, and community theatres to meld various segments of their communities that might not ordinarily respond to a nonmusical effort. For example, the incorporation of groups such as church choirs, dance schools, gymnastic teams, and folk dance clubs can lead to a successful and enjoyable experience for both producers and performers. In addition, these groups often introduce enthusiastic newcomers who prove invaluable to later, nonmusical productions. Many musicals offer maximum flexibility in terms of cast size. Choruses can be as large as the casting turnout allows. The chorus can easily include all ages, sizes, and ethnic backgrounds, as well as the handicapped and disabled. Finally, no other type of theatre projects the energy and vivacity of the production so happily to the community.

With all of these solid advantages to presenting a musical, the producing group should not let itself be deterred by the large physical scale, expense, and technical difficulties so often associated with musicals. There is no reason that a musical cannot be done imaginatively and artistically, if all of the elements for a successful production are prepared for well in advance. As a guideline for such preparation, we present a pattern for successfully producing a musical.

Chapter 1 deals with preliminary considerations on all production levels and offers practical advice and specific suggestions in the areas of production, play selection, casting, setting up and conducting rehearsals, scene design and execution, and costuming a show. Chapter 2 is an annotated listing of over three hundred musical plays coded to designate basic requirements and special concerns, as well as to indicate the companies that control amateur production rights. Chapter 3 is a directory of sources for information, materials, and supplies related to the production of musicals. Also included is a glossary of specialized terms, a bibliography of references on amateur theatrical production and on producing musicals, and an index.

PRODUCING THE MUSICAL

1

THE APPROACH

As in all types of theatre, money, people, and time play an important part in the preparation of a musical. The producing organization must learn to budget each of these elements both individually and collectively. If sufficient organization and forethought is practiced early in the planning period, the resulting production should benefit artistically and financially.

BUDGET: MONEY

The monetary budget for a show is of primary importance to the producing organization. As is true of most modern plays, a musical carries with it a production fee called a royalty. Only after a play enters the public domain does it cease to carry a royalty fee. For most nonmusicals, public domain begins seventy-five years after the death of the playwright, unless one is dealing with a modern translation or adaptation. Musicals, however, may be entailed much longer because royalties also govern musical arrangements, which may be updated from time to time, thus extending the time during which royalties must be paid. In addition, royalties for a musical are considerably higher than those for a nonmusical, usually running several hundred dollars for multiple performances. The royalty and music rental fee for a recent college production of *Carousel* with a six-night run in an auditorium seating eight hundred and with tickets at $4.00 and $2.50 was $2,460. Smaller shows and houses and shorter runs cost considerably less, but there is no denying that financial investment in the production of a musical is substantial and must be discussed thoroughly before launching a production. To determine the royalty fee for a musical, the producer must contact the organization that controls the amateur production rights for the show in question. The majority of American musicals are controlled by the following organizations: Tams-Witmark Music Library, Music Theatre International, the Rodgers and Hammerstein Library, Samuel French, and the Dramatic Publishing Company. In addition to these, several outstanding children's musical shows are handled by Anchorage Press, Baker's Plays, Performance Publishing Company, Coach House Press, and Pioneer Drama Service. Each of these organizations publishes a catalog that lists authors and composers and describes plots and musical numbers of shows whose rights they control. These catalogs are free upon request and may also be obtained from most libraries. Mailing addresses and telephone numbers for these organizations are listed in Chapter 3 of this volume.

Also upon request, but at a slight charge to cover mailing expense, the controlling organization will send the producing organization an advance script and musical score for perusal. A sample contract may be sent, detailing the specific costs and agreements that must be met by the producing organization if performances are to be held. In some cases a letter of agreement, such as the sample one that follows, is sent to the producing organization by the controlling company.

Sample Perusal Copy Letter 1

Dear [Organization]:

We have sent you perusal copies in accordance with your request. We know this valuable service will greatly help you in choosing your musical show.

Our financial quotation which is enclosed is based on your seating capacity and your ticket prices.

Our conditions of lease are contained on the enclosed information sheet. We also enclose a contract which we require completed, signed, and returned to us when ordering.

When returning your signed contract, please send us a purchase order or your check for the full royalty and rental of all material. In place of the purchase order we will accept the signature of your principal or chief administrator on our contract. If we do not receive a purchase order, your check, or our signed contract we will ship COD for the total royalty and rental.

We know that you will find the presentation of one of our quality musicals to be a richly rewarding activity.

Sincerely yours,

[Controlling Organization]

The producing organization is under no obligation at this time. Figures are presented by the controlling company for the producing organization to consider. Royalty costs will depend on several factors, such as the number of performances, the size of the performance hall, the price of the tickets, the type of orchestration desired (full orchestra, two pianos, and so forth), and the length of time the rented material will be required. Unlike non-musical scripts, which may be purchased, libretti for most musicals and the music itself for all musicals may only be rented for a given period of time (usually by the month) and must be cleaned of notation and returned to the controlling organization as soon as the final performance has been given. Obviously, any notations or directions made by the director, cast, or orchestra must be made lightly in pencil for easy erasing before the material is returned.

Some controlling organizations (Tams-Witmark, for example) often send "sides" instead of full scripts for the performers. A side consists of the cues and lines for a particular performer or character, deleting the lines of all other characters; hence, very few performers have the entire script for the show. The sides also contain only the stage directions pertinent to that particular character. Inexperienced actors often find the use of sides confusing and insufficient; therefore, the director must take care to organize and explain the material well from the first rehearsal in order to avoid chaos. The director may want to make a full script available for any performer who needs to consult it. Paperback versions of some musicals are available and, because of the expense of any lost rental scripts, it is often advisable to purchase them and use them instead of passing out the rental scripts. Most companies insist on the rental fee anyway, but the extra expense of buying paperbacks is worthwhile when one considers the cost of payment for lost rental sides and the confusion that often results from their use.

In addition to the royalty and rental fees, a production contract for a musical will carry a stipulation concerning the publicity for the agreed-upon performances. Although terms differ according to the specific company, essentially the producing organization must agree to list the authors, composers, and lyricists of the show in any written form of publicity, and to list these agents along with the controlling organization on the programs, and sometimes on posters, for the production. Copies of the contract must be signed and returned to the controlling organization before rehearsals for the show may begin. Copies of posters, programs, and publicity releases must be sent to the controlling organization under the terms of the contract. Producers should make these contractual commitments months in advance so that the rehearsal schedule will not be hampered.

A producer must uphold the agreements in the contract, as breaking the agreement constitutes an illegality for which the producer and the producing organization can be held liable. A sample contract, similar to one that might be sent to the amateur musical producer, follows. It is quite different from an agreement for a nonmusical, which does not involve formal contracts, and often comes as a shock to the novice musical producer. Sometimes it may seem to be intended as a deterrent to musical production, but it is a necessary addition. The entire *musical* part of a musical adds a complete new dimension which must be covered in a contract.

Sample Performance Contract

Agreement, Made on Behalf of the Copyright Proprietors,
to be Signed by Organizations and Schools
Performing Musical Shows or Renting Musical Material

We hereby agree to pay the rentals and royalties specified in your quotation letter relating to the performance of the musical work _____ [fill in title] on the spoken stage for _____ [fill in number of performances] performances on _____ [fill in dates] at _____ [fill in name of auditorium or hall, street address, city, and state]. The seating capacity of the above auditorium is _____ [fill in number of seats]. The admission prices to be charged are _____ [fill in prices]. The royalty and rental quotation given to us by the controlling organization is $_____ [fill in price] for the first performance and $_____ [fill in price] for each additional consecutive performance. To be considered consecutive each performance must be presented in the same auditorium and within seven days of the preceding performance.

All contemplated performances have been listed above. We agree that no changes can be made in the dates or number of performances, capacity or location of auditorium, and/or admission prices. We agree that should we desire any changes we will immediately request your approval, and that this may result in an increase in the royalty and rental prices quoted, if such changes are approved. We reserve the absolute right to approve or disapprove any desired changes or additions to this agreement. All changes or additions must be requested in writing and become effective only when approved by us in writing. We agree that we will not announce, advertise, or sell tickets for any additional performances until you have specifically licensed us to perform these additional performances.

All of the provisions of the enclosed sheet titled "Information Regarding the Rental of Music and Dialogue Material," including provisions on the reverse sides thereof, apply to this agreement and are made part hereof. We agree that the music and dialogue material will be returned to you, prepaid, within seven (7) days after the performance or performances and that the full replacement costs of all missing or mutilated material, additional royalty, and rental, and any charges in connection with this transaction, will be paid. We understand we are responsible for all material in transit, until it is delivered to you at your address.

The material rented to us shall not be copied, reproduced, sold, or otherwise distributed by us or with our permission, and shall be used only for the purpose of giving the performances above specified.

The acknowledgment hereof or shipment of the material to us will constitute this a valid agreement between us.

Check here if you will use an orchestration._____.

We will want to rent the orchestration for a total of _____ [fill in number] months before the first performance.

Check here if you will not use an orchestration. _____

We will want to rent the rehearsal material for a total of _____ [fill in number] months before the first performance.

PLEASE MAKE AND KEEP A COPY OF THIS AGREEMENT SO THAT YOU CAN NOTIFY US PROMPTLY SHOULD ANY OF THE INFORMATION YOU HAVE FILLED IN CHANGE.

_____
Name of Organization

_____
Signature & Title

**Information Regarding the Rental of Music and Dialogue
Material of Musical Shows for Stage Performance**

The material we furnish of a musical show consists of the MUSIC and DIALOGUE. The music and dialogue that are included in the rental charge given in our quotation letter comprise:

1. One score for use by the conductor. (This is a piano-conductor score. Orchestra scores [full scores] are not available for musical comedies and operettas.)
2. Vocal parts for the principal singers.
3. Twenty-five chorus books.
4. One prompt book, containing the complete dialogue.
5. Dialogue parts (sides) for the speaking characters.

The rehearsal material (as listed in paragraphs 1, 2, 3, 4, and 5 above) is loaned for a period of three (3) months. However, the rehearsal material is to be returned within seven (7) days after the last performance regardless of when it was originally received, even if less than a three-month period has expired. Should the rehearsal material be required for longer than three months, there is an additional rental charge of sixty dollars ($60.00) per month.

SHOULD YOU REQUIRE ORCHESTRA PARTS FOR THE SHOW, YOU MUST CHECK THE APPROPRIATE BOX ON THE AGREEMENT FORM, AND INDICATE THE NUMBER OF MONTHS YOU REQUIRE THE ORCHESTRATION. THERE IS A RENTAL CHARGE OF NINETY-FIVE DOLLARS ($95.00) PER MONTH FOR THE ORCHESTRATION. Should you require the orchestration, it must be rented for a period commencing a minimum of one month prior to the first performance. Should performances continue over a period of more than one calendar week (Monday through Sunday), additional orchestration rental will be charged, prorated by the one-quarter month.

Extra orchestra parts (we supply strings 2-1-1-1-1) rent for eight dollars ($8.00) each per month.

The Stage Manager's Guide, which contains some helpful staging information, is not part of the ordinary rehearsal material, but can be obtained for many shows at an extra rental of thirty-five dollars ($35.00) for any part of a three-month period.

Additional prompt books rent for four dollars ($4.00) each for a three-month period. Additional conductor's scores, if published, rent for eight dollars ($8.00) each for a three-month period or, if manuscript, rent for twelve dollars ($12.00) each for a three-month period. If more than twenty-five chorus books are required, there is an additional rental charge of three dollars ($3.00) for each additional copy for a three-month period. Should any of the above additional material be needed for more than a three-month period, the rental for the extra time will be prorated on a monthly basis. However, there is no reduction in the three-month rate should the additional material not be needed for the full three months.

THE RENTAL OF ALL REHEARSAL MATERIALS, ORCHESTRATIONS, ADDITIONAL MATERIAL BEYOND THE MATERIALS NORMALLY SUPPLIED, AND MATERIALS FOR ADDITIONAL PERIODS OF TIME IS DEPENDENT UPON AVAILABILITY. Therefore, please inform us as early as possible concerning material required, so we can make every effort to supply you. The licensee must report, in writing, any error or deficiency in material received within seven (7) days after receipt of the material.

All material must be returned to the library within seven (7) days after the last performance. Additional rental charges in the above amounts will be made for material returned more than seven (7) days after the last performance. When returning material, always wrap securely, insure sufficiently, and mark the wrapper with the name of your organization so we can issue proper credit. The licensee is responsible for all material while it is in transit both ways. IT IS UNDERSTOOD THAT THE LICENSEE PAYS ALL SHIPPING CHARGES ON PACKAGES BOTH WAYS. THE LICENSEE PAYS ALL TELEGRAPH AND ALL TELEPHONE CHARGES PERTAINING TO THE RENTAL AND SHIPMENT OF MATERIAL. THE LICENSEE PAYS ALL BROKERAGE AND ENTRY CHARGES BOTH WAYS ON FOREIGN SHIPMENTS. FOREIGN SHIPMENTS MUST BE SHIPPED BY AIR TRANSPORTATION BOTH WAYS, AT THE LICENSEE'S EXPENSE.

The rights to the musical show include the use of the music, lyrics, and story as composed and written by the authors and supplied by us to the licensee. The licensee agrees to make no additions, transpositions, or interpolations of any kind in, and no substantial deletions from, the music score or book. The rights granted to the licensee do not include any right to the original choreography, original direction or staging, original costume designs, or original scenery designs.

The names of the authors of the musical show and other credits appearing in our catalog must appear in a prominent place on the title page of the program and in all billings of the Play in such form as they are printed in our catalog. We require a line on the title page of the program stating that the musical show is produced by arrangement with, and the music and dialogue material furnished by, us. We require one copy of this program of the show.

The licensee agrees that it will not directly or indirectly assign or sublicense any of the rights granted to it.

The right to radio broadcast, telecast, or record the material in any manner is not included.

ALL MATERIAL MUST BE RETURNED IN GOOD CONDITION. CUTS MUST BE MADE LIGHTLY AND ONLY IN SOFT BLACK LEAD PENCIL. REPLACEMENT CHARGE WILL BE MADE FOR ANY MATERIAL CUT OR MARKED IN COLORED PENCIL, CRAYON, OR INK OR WATER SOAKED. CUTS AND ALL OTHER NOTATIONS MUST BE ERASED FROM ALL REHEARSAL MATERIAL AND ORCHESTRATIONS BEFORE THEY ARE RETURNED. A CHARGE WILL BE MADE IF THE MATERIAL IS RETURNED DIRTY. REPLACEMENT CHARGES WILL BE MADE FOR MUTILATED AND LOST MATERIAL. WE APPRECIATE YOUR COOPERATION IN CARING FOR THE RENTAL MATERIAL.

This material is usually accompanied by a letter stating royalty and rental charges, an example of which follows.

Sample Perusal Copy Letter 2

Dear [Organization]:

We recently sent you copies of musical show material to consider for stage performance. We know you have found this perusal service valuable. Your royalty and rental quotation was:

Royalty and rental for first performance	Charge for each additional consecutive performance
$_____	$_____

The above quotation is based on a seating capacity of _____ with tickets priced at $_____.

Should you now have decided to present a show, please return your contract so we can schedule shipment of the material to you. We are enclosing an additional contract in case you have misplaced the first one. When you have returned your contract, you may keep, at no extra charge, until after your performances, the book and score of the show you will present.

We will be pleased to send books and scores of any additional shows you would like to study, should you not yet have been able to pick the production that is best for your group.

You will find the form below useful in replying to us. Should you have any questions about placing your order, you may write on the back of this sheet.

Sincerely yours,

[Controlling Organization]

_____ I am returning herewith my signed and completed contract for presentation of _____.

_____ I would like perusal copies of _____.

Please return this sheet with your reply so we can identify your account. Please do not return unsigned contracts.

While contracts are basically the same, they do vary somewhat among controlling organizations with regard to form and costs. Here is another example of a contract the producer might receive.

Sample License

LICENSE TO   DATE _____
                                        PLAY _____
GENTLEMEN:

We hereby license you to present the Play indicated above, upon the following terms and conditions:

1. Place of presentation _____
2. Number of performances _____
3. (a) ROYALTY (for the performance of the Play only): _____.
   (b) All sums to be paid us as royalties under this license are to be held by you in trust for us until actually received by us. This trust relationship shall not be open to question or challenge by you by reason of your failure physically to segregate such sums or to commit any other act that might otherwise jeopardize such relationship.
   (c) You shall submit to us, within five days following demand by us, a sworn statement setting forth the total number of performances actually presented and the precise date and place of each such performance.
   (d) In consideration of the grant by us to you of the right to present the Play, it is understood that even if you do not present the Play for any reason whatsoever, you shall nevertheless be obligated to pay us the amount of the guaranteed ROYALTY set forth in subparagraph (a) above.
   (e) You shall bill the Play and the Author(s) in all programs, houseboards, displays, and in all other advertising announcements in the following manner:
                        Author(s) name(s)
                        Show Title
4. MATERIAL
   (a) RENTAL FEE: $_____ for use of materials, to be paid on the signing of this license.
   (b) You shall be responsible to us for the safe return of all the rented material. Any damage to or loss of the material prior to its return to us shall be evaluated by us and charged to you; you agree upon demand promptly to reimburse us for the full amount of such evaluated damage to or loss of material.
   (c) In consideration of our having reserved the material especially for your production, it is understood that even if you do not present the Play, you shall nevertheless be obligated to pay us the amount of the rental fee set forth in subparagraph (a) above.

(d) The material to be furnished to you hereunder shall consist in its entirety of the following: _____. We make no representation that the material indicated above is adequate for your needs nor any representation as to the condition of the material.

NOTE: The granting of this license to you to perform the Play is not to be construed as a right to interpolate new music or lyrics or changes, or alter any music or lyrics or anything in the text included with the rented material. No changes of any kind shall be made in the Play including but not limited to the deletion or interpolation of new music, lyrics, or dialogue in the presently existing Play. You are not permitted to make any copies of the material or to alter, amend, or change it without written consent. YOU ARE PROHIBITED FROM RECORDING, REPRODUCING, TELEVISING, OR BROAD-CASTING THE PLAY OR ANY PORTION OF IT BY ANY MEANS WHATSOEVER. Any violation hereof will be deemed a willful infringement of the copyright of the Authors. This license does not include the right to the original choreography.

(e) You shall pay transportation charges BOTH WAYS for the material rented to you herein, as well as all customs charges, duties, and similar imposts in connection with shipments of materials outside of the United States and return shipments to us. Any expense we are required to incur with respect to the delivery or return of the material shall be charged to you; you agree upon demand promptly to reimburse us for the full amount of such expense.

(f) You understand that the material will not be used for any pur-pose other than as stated herein. You agree that NO LATER THAN SEVEN DAYS AFTER THE LAST PERFORMANCE HEREUNDER you will return to us, by prepaid express, insured for not less than two hundred fifty ($250.00) dollars, the com-plete material (including any material added by you) in as good condition as when the material was turned over to you. Should you fail to return the complete material to us as herein provided, we shall be entitled to an additional rental fee of ten ($10.00) dollars for each day any material is retained by you beyond the period of seven days after the last performance.

5. All payments are to be made by check to us.

6. You shall give appropriate credit to us in your programs. You shall forward at least one (1) copy of the program of your production to us not later than three (3) days following the opening performance licensed hereunder. We warrant that on behalf of the owners of the copyright in the Play, we are authorized to grant this license to you. We make no other warranties.

(a) You shall keep and maintain full and regular books and records wherein shall be recorded all items in connection with the production and presentation of the Play, including all monies received and all monies expended. Such books and records shall be open at all regular business hours for inspection by us and our representative at your office, and we shall have the right to make copies thereof and take extracts therefrom and to inspect daily box office records and receipts for the purpose of verifying the accuracy of all statements rendered and sums paid hereunder.

(b) This license shall automatically terminate in the event that you default in performing any of the obligations imposed upon you.

By_____

Amateur producers may find themselves dismayed by the legal jargon in these production contracts and be tempted to cancel the entire project. At this point they must take heart, however, and remember that many others before them have struggled with the terms and gone on to present highly successful productions. It is really to the producer's advantage to have the companies detail all specific costs and instructions in advance—so there are no surprises—and for that reason the producing organization should study the agreement carefully and weigh all considerations before proceeding with production plans. Because musical agencies insist on their rental fees and their royalties *before* any rehearsal material is sent, budget money for musicals must be set aside well in advance of production.

BUDGET: PEOPLE

A second area of major importance for the producer of the nonprofessional musical is people—there is a large personnel difference between a nonmusical and a musical production. This difference involves not only expense but also increased supporting staff, additional rehearsal time and space, and the variety of possible musical accompaniment. Figures 1 and 2 demonstrate the organization of production staffs for a musical and a nonmusical, clearly demonstrating the differences between the production types. A definition of each staff position in both, including musical and nonmusical staffs, and an outline of responsibilities follow.

The *producing agency* furnishes funds for producing the season's plays and for the production staff or director, scene designer, costumer, and technical director if they are paid positions. All committees must stay within the budgets established by the producing agency. Examples of producing agencies include a high school or college, a community theatre group, a community agency such as a parks and recreation program, or a local or area arts council.

The *director* is primarily responsible for the stylistic concept of the production, for its staging, and for unifying the technical elements

Figure 1. Production Staff for Musicals

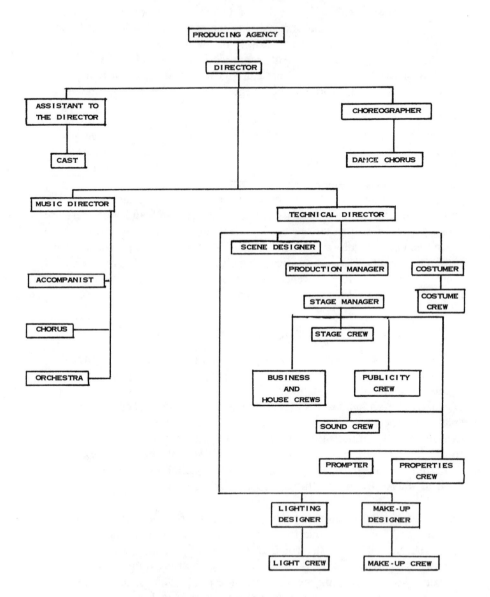

Figure 2. Production Staff for Nonmusicals

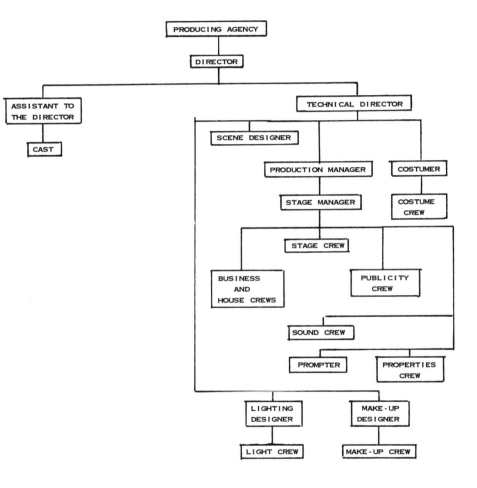

into a cohesive whole. The director may or may not be involved in the technical aspects of the production (for example, set design, costume design) or in areas in addition to the staging (for example, choreography), depending upon personal choice or qualifications.

The *assistant to the director* acts as liaison between the director and the various heads of crews, takes notes for and on the show during rehearsals, keeps a list of cast and crew addresses and telephone numbers, and keeps a production chart of work in progress. The assistant director also stands in at rehearsal for anyone who is missing—such as an actor or stage manager. In addition, the assistant director may conduct minirehearsals of special groups (a children's chorus, for instance) while the director is working with another group.

The *music director* interprets and rehearses all vocal and instrumental music for the production and may also serve as conductor for the orchestra.

The *accompanist* is the individual who serves as pianist during the rehearsal period. The accompanist may or may not play in the orchestra during performances.

The *chorus* identifies all cast members who are not designated as individualized characters but who appear and sing as a group in musical numbers.

The *orchestra* consists of the instrumentalists who play for the performers. The number of orchestra members can vary widely according to the demands of the show and to the availability of talented musicians.

The *choreographer* designs the dance movements for the production and may be responsible for the staging of musical numbers.

The *dance chorus* identifies those performers whose primary responsibility is the dance movement in the musical numbers. They may or may not sing with the chorus.

The *technical director* is responsible for the overall technical design and construction of a production (set, lights, sound, properties, special effects), unless certain of these areas are the responsibility of a designer or the director. The technical director is also responsible for maintaining the theatre's work areas and for inventorying, maintaining, and ordering all necessary technical equipment, such as hand tools, lumber, scenic canvas and paint, color gelatin for stage lights, and any type of stage hardware needed for a production. Several crew heads may therefore work under the direct supervision of the technical director.

The *scene designer* is responsible for the overall set design for the production, providing the director with a scaled floorplan and a color rendering or scaled model of the design. Elements of line, mass, and color are taken into account in the design.

The *production manager* acts as liaison between the technical director and various heads of crews, and takes notes for and on the progress of the technical work. The production manager also keeps a list of addresses and telephone numbers of crew members, and a production chart of the work in progress.

The *stage manager* acts as the representative of the technical director and director during the actual running of a production. During rehearsals, the stage manager compiles a script containing blocking notations, sound and light cues, and curtain warnings, and also compiles a list of furniture and props necessary for each scene. During the run of the show, the stage manager is responsible for giving all cues and directing all set changes as well as for posting rehearsal times and director's notes.

The *stage crew* is responsible for scenery construction and painting, and for running the set changes during the show. Crew members are directly under the supervision of the technical director and the production manager.

The *costumer* is responsible for the overall costume design of a production (unless relieved of that responsibility by a director or scene designer) as well as for the construction of the costumes. The costumer also supervises all costume-related inventorying, maintenance of equipment, and ordering of materials.

The *costume crew* is responsible for itemizing the costumes and costume pieces necessary for a production, pulling costumes from stock or constructing new ones, and making an inventory of costumes following each production. Crew members are responsible for measuring the cast members and keeping a measurement file of all performers. During production they are responsible for cleaning, laundering, and pressing the costume items used in the show. The costume crew is under the supervision of the costumer.

The *business and house crews* are responsible for the printing of tickets (checking play title, dates, and seat numbers for ticket copy). They set up a box office staff to take telephone reservations and to sell tickets both in advance of the opening and on production nights. They arrange time schedules for the box office staff, and are responsible for obtaining seating charts of the theatre on which sales must be recorded. They also arrange for the use of the theatre for the nights of production, set up a schedule for opening the theatre on those nights, and make arrangements with the stage manager for holding the curtain (if necessary) and for the seating of latecomers. Finally, they secure an ushering staff and are responsible for instructing this staff in seating procedures.

The *publicity crew* is responsible for the overall publicity scheme of a play. It is suggested that crew members develop an easily recognizable logo for the show which will help unify posters, programs, and newspaper ads. The publicity crew is further responsible for news releases to newspapers, public service announcements (PSAs) to local radio stations, copy and design for both posters and programs, and arrangements for the taking of all photographs. The distribution of all posters, as well as the planning of special events related to the production—such as a reception—also falls under their jurisdiction.

The *sound crew* is responsible for ordering new materials, maintaining and repairing sound equipment during the run of the show, operating the sound equipment during the performances, and inventorying all equipment at the end of each production. Before the production opens, the sound crew checks the sound systems for malfunctions and, during rehearsals, prepares a plan of action to be followed in case of problems. The sound crew is also responsible for checking the sound equipment before *each* performance. It is suggested that, if space permits, a file of records and sound tapes from previous productions be maintained.

A *prompter* is of primary value at the point in the rehearsal period when the actors put aside their scripts and begin to rely on memorization. If other duties permit, the assistant director may fill this position; however, in a large-cast show it may be preferable to have a separate individual to give cues and take notes on weak areas. In general, a prompter is not necessary during actual production. Experience has shown, also, that actors give more unified performances when they depend on each other for help in trouble spots. Of course, the director may decide either way. In any case, it is advisable to have someone follow the script during all rehearsals and performances to note sections where actors veer from the script or have particular problems with it.

The *properties crew* list all stage and hand props for the production, find sources for obtaining either props or the materials for constructing them, list each borrowed item by the name and address of the owner, clean and care for each, and see to the proper return of each following the production. They coordinate props to the show in terms of production style, color, and period. They are responsible for any stage item not part of the set, setting up and maintaining appropriate hand-prop tables backstage, locating stage furniture, changing stage props and furnishings at intermission, repairing any damaged items, and inventorying the prop room following each show.

The *lighting designer* establishes the production's light design after consulting with the director, the technical director, and the set designer.

The *light crew* is responsible for hanging and focusing all lighting instruments, inventorying lighting materials and equipment after each production, maintaining equipment, and ordering new equipment. This crew operates the lights for each performance, checks them well before performance time, and outlines an alternate lighting scheme in case of lighting failures.

The *makeup designer* is responsible for makeup design and application. The makeup designer designs the makeup on appropriate charts after meeting with the technical director and costumer.

The *makeup crew* is responsible for makeup inventories, for setting up the makeup rooms and cleaning and maintaining them, and for the early preparation of any items of special difficulty to a show (wigs, beards, and so forth). They are responsible for helping inexperienced actors with the application of makeup on nights of performance, and for the care and period-styling of wigs.

Combinations of staff positions are quite possible. A director may, for example, also be a choreographer or a musical director, or both. A technical director may also be able to design both costumes and scenery. To achieve the most unified production possible, however, it is best to consider the staff positions that must be filled and the available personnel before the combinations are set.

Musical accompaniment can be handled in various ways. It is becoming increasingly popular to use tapes, specially marketed, with the full instrumental accompaniment for the best-known shows. These tapes usually have the music recorded at two different tempos, one a slower rehearsal speed and the other a regular show tempo. Live musical accompaniment is preferable, however, regardless of whether it is of professional calibre. We would usually rather see and hear a musical with inexperienced live musicians, and all the attendant bloopers, than listen to a perfect but prerecorded musical score. No matter how sophisticated and extensive the original orchestration of a musical may have been, it is possible to reduce a full orchestra to two pianos, a piano and organ (an instrument with a rich variety of simulated orchestral sounds), a piano and drums, or a small combination of piano, violin, horn, and drums. Certain shows, such as *The Boy Friend* and *The Me Nobody Knows*, are written for small combos, and many of the most popular musical productions (*Little Mary Sunshine* and *The Fantasticks*, for example) were first produced off-Broadway and were scored for one- or two-piano accompaniment.

BUDGET: TIME

Just as the budgeting of money and people is important to the producer, so is the budgeting of time. A musical requires not only more rehearsal time

than a nonmusical, but also different types of rehearsals. Separate
times must be allotted for scene-staging rehearsals, chorus rehearsals,
choreography rehearsals, and orchestra rehearsals. In early weeks
it is quite conceivable that two or more of these types of rehearsals
may be scheduled simultaneously, if space and manpower permit. In such
scheduling the director must be careful not to schedule the same person in
two rehearsals at once. Once again, the need for maximum preproduction
organization by the producer and director becomes obvious. Although there
are several valid ways of scheduling rehearsals for a musical, we offer the
following examples (one for a comparatively small musical and one for a
large-scale show) as workable schedules and include the schedule of a nonmusical for contrast. We might note that the length of the rehearsal period
for a musical will vary according to the experience of the producing organization, the difficulty of the particular show, and the amount of time spent
in each rehearsal period. There can be no doubt, however, that a musical
will require more rehearsals than a nonmusical, although the time spent in
"polishing" the show is much greater for the nonmusical. In addition, a
large-cast musical will require a different rehearsal schedule than a small-
cast musical. It should be noted too that nonprofessionals generally have
neither the power of concentration nor the physical stamina for more than
three hours of rehearsing until final run-throughs. Most three-hour
rehearsals should include a twenty-minute break.

Sample Small-Cast Musical Rehearsal Schedule: *The Boy Friend*

Friday, June 24	7:00-9:30 P.M.	Block Act I
Saturday, June 25	9:30-11:30 A.M.	"Won't You Charleston"
	11:30-1:00 P.M.	"Boy Friend"—all
Sunday, June 26	4:30-7:30 P.M.	Act I, repeat Block Act II (half)
Monday, June 27	6:45 P.M.	"Won't You Charleston"
	7:00-9:30 P.M.	Act II, repeat and finish
Tuesday, June 28	7:00-9:30 P.M.	Block Act III
Wednesday, June 29	6:45 P.M.	"Boyfriend"
	7:00-9:30 P.M.	Repeat Acts I, II (half)
Thursday, June 30	7:00-9:30 P.M.	Repeat Acts II (half), III
Friday, July 1	4:00-6:00 P.M.	"Sur La Plage"
	6:00-8:00 P.M.	"Safety in Numbers"
**Saturday, July 2	9:30-11:30 A.M.	"I Could Be Happy"
	11:30-1:30 P.M.	"Riviera"
	4:30-7:30 P.M.	Review ALL musical numbers

**Sunday, July 3	7:00-9:30 P.M.	Dances and musical numbers, Acts II, III, review and work spots —musical numbers
Monday, July 4	6:30 P.M.	Review "Boyfriend" and "Safety in Numbers" "Riviera"
Tuesday, July 5	6:30 P.M.	Review Act II dances
	7:00-9:30 P.M.	Acts I (lines and musical numbers), II (half)
Wednesday, July 6	7:00-9:30 P.M.	"Riviera"
	7:00-9:30 P.M.	Acts II (lines and musical numbers), III
Wednesday, July 6	7:00-9:30 P.M.	Whole show walk-through, lights
Thursday, July 7	7:00-9:30 P.M.	Act III (lines) Review "Riviera," work what is needed
Friday, July 8	7:00-9:30 P.M.	Act III (lines) Review "Riviera"
Saturday, July 9	Hold open	Work what is needed
**Sunday, July 10	4:30-7:30 P.M.	To be announced
Monday, July 11	7:30-10:00 P.M.	Act I PROPS
Tuesday, July 12	7:30-10:00 P.M.	Act II PROPS
Wednesday, July 13	7:30-10:00 P.M.	Act III PROPS
Thursday, July 14	7:00-10:00 P.M.	Whole show (costumes)
Friday, July 15	7:30-10:00 P.M.	Technical rehearsal NO ACTORS
Saturday, July 16	7:30-10:30 P.M.	First dress (no makeup)
Sunday, July 17	2:30-4:30 P.M.	Pace rehearsal
*Sunday, July 17	7:00-10:30 P.M.	Dress rehearsal (no makeup)
*Monday, July 18	6:30 P.M.	Makeup—first dress
*Tuesday, July 19	6:30 P.M.	Second dress—pictures
*Wednesday, July 20	6:30 P.M.	Third dress
*Thursday, July 21	6:30 P.M.	Makeup for 8:00 P.M. performance
Friday, July 22	6:30 P.M.	Makeup for 8:00 P.M. performance
*Saturday, July 23	6:30 P.M.	Makeup for 7:15 P.M. performance
	9:30 P.M.	Buffet and dance
**Wednesday, July 27	7:30 P.M.	Brush-up rehearsal (no costumes, no makeup)

*Thursday, July 28	6:30 P.M.	Makeup for 8:00 P.M. performance
*Friday, July 29	6:30 P.M.	Makeup for 8:00 P.M. performance
*Saturday, July 30	6:30 P.M.	Makeup for 8:00 P.M. performance
Sunday, July 31	4:00 P.M.	STRIKE CALL AND PICNIC

*EXCLUSIVE of individual and group vocal periods.
**From this point on, until July 14, songs and dances are done first, then the whole act, including songs and dances—thus limiting polishing time greatly.

Sample Large-Cast Musical Rehearsal Schedule: *Carousel*

BR = BAND ROOM
CR = CHORAL ROOM
DS = DANCE STUDIO
MS = MAIN STAGE
RS = REHEARSAL STAGE

Monday, March 14	6:30 P.M.	Read-through (MS)
Monday, March 28	7:30 P.M.	Block Iii (RS)
Tuesday, March 29	7:00 P.M.	Children's chorus (CR)
	7:30 P.M.	Adult chorus (CR)
	7:30 P.M.	Children (MS)
Wednesday, March 30	7:30 P.M.	Block Iiii (MS) NO CHORUS
Thursday, March 31	7:30 P.M.	"June Is Bustin' " (DS) DANCERS ONLY
	7:30 P.M.	Billy and Julie (RS)
Sunday, April 3	5:00 P.M.	Block Ii (MS)
Monday, April 4	7:30 P.M.	Block IIiii, IIvi (MS) NO CHORUS
Tuesday, April 5	7:00 P.M.	Children's chorus (CR)
	7:30 P.M.	Adult chorus (CR)
	7:30 P.M.	Children (RS)
	8:30 P.M.	Block IIv (RS)
Wednesday, April 6	7:30 P.M.	Block IIi, IIii (MS)
Thursday, April 7	7:30 P.M.	"June Is Bustin' " (DS) DANCERS ONLY
	8:30 P.M.	"Hornpipe" (DS) DANCERS ONLY
	7:30 P.M.	Billy and Julie (RS)

Sunday, April 10	5:00 P.M.	Review Ii (MS) Block Iiii (chorus sections)
Monday, April 11	7:30 P.M.	Iii, IIiii, IIvi (DS) NO CHORUS
Tuesday, April 12	7:00 P.M.	Children's chorus (CR)
	7:30 P.M.	Adult chorus (CR)
	7:30 P.M.	Children (RS)
	7:30 P.M.	IIv (MS)
Wednesday, April 13	7:30 P.M.	Iiii (RS) NO CHORUS
	8:30 P.M.	IIi, IIii NO CHORUS
Thursday, April 14	7:30 P.M.	IIiv (RS)
Sunday, April 17	5:00 P.M.	Block IIi, IIii, IIvi (MS)

FROM THIS POINT, NO SCRIPTS OR MUSIC MAY BE USED
  ONSTAGE.
ALL LINES AND LYRICS ARE TO BE MEMORIZED.

Monday, April 18	7:30 P.M.	Iiii (RS)
Tuesday, April 19	7:30 P.M.	Children's chorus (CR)
	7:30 P.M.	Adult chorus (CR)
	7:30 P.M.	Children (RS)
Wednesday, April 20	7:30 P.M.	Iiii (RS) NO CHORUS
	8:00 P.M.	IIi NO CHORUS
	9:00 P.M.	IIii NO CHORUS
Thursday, April 21	7:30 P.M.	IIiv (DS) DANCERS
	8:30 P.M.	"June Is Bustin' " DANCERS ONLY
	9:15 P.M.	"Hornpipe" DANCERS ONLY
Sunday, April 24	5:00 P.M.	Ii, Iiii (MS) CHORUS SECTION
	6:00 P.M.	IIi, IIii, IIvi CHORUS SECTION
Monday, April 25	7:30 P.M.	Iii (RS)
	9:00 P.M.	IIiii
Tuesday, April 26	6:30 P.M.	Adult chorus (CR)
	7:00 P.M.	Iiii (including chorus and dancers) (RS)

Wednesday, April 27	7:00 P.M.	IIi (including chorus) (RS)
	8:00 P.M.	IIiii
Thursday, April 28	7:00 P.M.	IIiv (DS)
	8:00 P.M.	"June Is Bustin' " DANCERS ONLY "Blow High, Blow Low" and "Hornpipe"
Friday, April 29	1:00 P.M.	"If I Loved You" and Soliloquy" (RS)
Sunday, May 1	4:30 P.M.	Adult chorus (CR)
	5:00 P.M.	I, run-through (MS)
Monday, May 2	7:00 P.M.	II, run-through (MS)
Tuesday, May 3	7:00 P.M.	I, run-through (MS)
Wednesday, May 4	7:00 P.M.	II, run-through (MS)
Thursday, May 5	7:00 P.M.	Run-through (MS)
Friday, May 6		To be announced
Sunday, May 8	2:00 P.M.	Orchestra (BR) Shift rehearsal (MS)
	6:00 P.M.	Run-through (MS)
Monday, May 9	7:00 P.M.	Run-through with orchestra (MS)
Tuesday, May 10	7:00 P.M.	Full dress rehearsal (MS)
Wednesday, May 11	7:00 P.M.	Final dress rehearsal (MS) with invited audience
Thursday, May 12	8:15 P.M.	OPENING NIGHT PERFORMANCE
Friday, May 13	8:15 P.M.	Performance
Saturday, May 14	8:15 P.M.	Performance
Wednesday, May 18	7:00 P.M.	Photo call
Thursday, May 19	8:15 P.M.	Performance
Friday, May 20	8:15 P.M.	Performance
Saturday, May 21	8:15 P.M.	Closing performance STRIKE, cast/crew party

Sample Nonmusical Rehearsal Schedule: *Dracula*

Friday, September 30	7:00-10:00 P.M.	Block Act I
Saturday, October 1	4:00-7:00 P.M.	Repeat Act I, Block Act II (first half)

Sunday, October 2	4:00-7:00 P.M.	Block Act II (second half)
Monday, October 3	7:00-10:00 P.M.	Block Act III
Tuesday, October 4	7:00-10:00 P.M.	Brush-up blocking
Wednesday, October 5	7:00-10:00 P.M.	Act I
Thursday, October 6	7:00-10:00 P.M.	Act II
Friday, October 7	7:00-10:00 P.M.	Act III
Saturday, October 8	4:00-7:00 P.M.	Whole show, walk-through for lights
Sunday, October 9	4:00-7:00 P.M.	Act I (lines)
Monday, October 10	7:00-10:00 P.M.	Acts I, II (half) (lines)
Tuesday, October 11	7:00-10:00 P.M.	Act II (lines)
Wednesday, October 12	7:00-10:00 P.M.	Acts I, II (lines)
Thursday, October 13	7:00-10:00 P.M.	Act III (lines)
Friday, October 14	7:00-10:00 P.M.	Acts I, II (half) ALL PROPS
Saturday, October 15	4:00-7:00 P.M.	Acts II (half), III ALL PROPS FROM NOW ON
Sunday, October 16		OFF
Monday, October 17	7:00-10:00 P.M.	Acts I, II (half) Set and furniture
Tuesday, October 18	7:00-10:00 P.M.	Acts II, III Set and furniture
Wednesday, October 19	7:00-10:00 P.M.	Costume, all sound cues rehearsed with actors
Thursday, October 20	7:00-11:00 P.M.	Whole show, notes
Friday, October 21	7:30 P.M.	Technical rehearsal, no actors
Saturday, October 22	7:30 P.M.	Run-through, costumes
Sunday, October 23	12:00-2:00 P.M.	Pace rehearsal, full dress
Monday, October 24	7:30 P.M.	Dress, with pictures
Tuesday, October 25	7:30 P.M.	Dress
Wednesday, October 26	8:00 P.M.	Invited dress
Thursday, October 27	8:00 P.M.	First performance
Friday, October 28	7:15 P.M.	Performance
Saturday, October 29	8:00 P.M.	Performance
Monday, October 31	10:30 A.M.	Matinee
Thursday, November 3	8:00 P.M.	Performance
Friday, November 4	8:00 P.M.	Performance
Saturday, November 5	8:00 P.M.	Performance
Sunday, November 6	4:00-7:00 P.M.	STRIKE PARTY

CHOOSING THE MUSICAL

There are three criteria to use when choosing a musical. First, the producing organization should consider the appeal a particular play will have for the audience in question. Certain plays, such as *The Boy Friend*, remain consistently popular with audiences everywhere, but an audience with a strong military background may well prefer *South Pacific* to *My Fair Lady*. Factors to be considered when analyzing the audience include age; sex; religious, educational, and economic background; any common group interests; and playgoing experience.

The tendency to produce only musicals with blockbuster titles is often strong among amateur theatre groups. It should be kept in mind, however, that these well-known shows offer two potential problems. First, they are often among the most difficult and spectacular shows to produce in terms of singing, dancing, or technical requirements. Second, their very popularity invites audiences to compare the local production with the professional stage or film version. Not surprisingly, the amateur production usually suffers in such a comparison. Finally, and quite aside from these two potential problems, it is always conceivable that an audience has grown tired of seeing the same familiar shows being done year after year and would actually prefer a less familiar show with a fresh approach. Most audiences enjoy being a part of a production that introduces them to new talent or new types of talent, new staging techniques, and new directorial or other ideas that enhance their enjoyment of musical theatre. The producer should both entertain an audience and offer them new challenges and insights into the art of theatre.

A second criterion the producer should consider when selecting a musical is the relationship, or "fit," between the requirements of the play script and the physical facility in which the show is to be staged. The size, shape, seating arrangement, and general condition of the performance hall may lend themselves more to an intimate ensemble show with piano and drums than to a large spectacle with a full orchestra. One would be foolish to choose a dance-oriented show for an auditorium with severely limited performance space. (Further discussion of this relationship may be found under the heading "Directing the Musical.")

Along the same lines, the producer should analyze the playing and backstage areas in terms of space and equipment. A fly gallery (a scenery-shifting system set above the stage) is of particular benefit in staging musicals. Backdrops and scenic pieces that can be easily flown in and out can save much time and space when the play shifts quickly from one scene to another, especially in shows like *The Music Man, Camelot,* and *Bye Bye Birdie*, with their highly episodic scripts. Wing space is likewise an important factor, particularly when a fly gallery system is not available. Remember that any piece of scenery used onstage must have a backstage storage spot when it is not in use on the stage. This problem is compounded when wing space must be shared by a large cast or crew. Finally, the placement of an orchestra can be a spatial problem in a performance hall without an orchestra pit. If backstage or auditorium space is required for the musicians, this space must be included in all designs and plans from the beginning.

A third important criterion the producer should consider when selecting a show is available talent. Usually, with some thought, the producer can recognize the amount and type of talent that will be available for a production. Far too often, however, a novice producer selects a play with no thought of any of the former criteria, but rather because he or she enjoys the tunes or because Barbra Streisand was superb in the film version. It is far more sensible—and necessary for the success of the show—to choose a particular play because the roles in it suit the available performers. Musicals can be categorized according to the special demands made on the performers, and the following categories are offered as guidelines for the producer or others when they are choosing a show with available talent in mind. These classifications also appear in the comprehensive list of individual musicals, which constitutes Chapter 2 of this book.

Star show (ST). A show written to showcase one or two characters, with these characters appearing in most musical numbers. The plot revolves so strongly around the stars that other characters can become extraneous. Cases in point include *Funny Girl, The Music Man, George M.,* and *They're Playing Our Song.* Producers should avoid star shows, or star vehicles, unless they are sure of having performers with extensive talent. One cannot simply expect an actor or actress of the proper calibre to play a Fanny Brice, George M. Cohan, or Harold Hill to show up unexpectedly at auditions.

Women's show (W). A show in which the majority of roles, leading and supporting, are female. Caution: Often a show built around a female character will actually have very few other female roles. *Annie Get Your Gun* and *The Unsinkable Molly Brown* are good examples of such shows.

Men's show (M). A show in which the majority of roles, leading and supporting, are male. The irony here is that although most auditions for amateur shows produce more women than men, most plays, musical and nonmusical, require more men than women performers.

Ensemble show (E). A show in which the roles and musical numbers are fairly evenly divided between male and female characters.

Children's show (CH). A show with important child characters, or a show in which children can easily be added to the required cast.

Dance show (D). A show with major emphasis on physical action and difficult dance sections that cannot be omitted without seriously altering the tone and impact of the show.

Singers' show (SNG). A show with major emphasis on superior singing ability and trained voices. This type of show may require such ability or training of the entire cast, as in *The Student Prince* and *Porgy and Bess*, or it may be restricted to specific characters, as in *My Fair Lady* and *South Pacific.*

Intimate show (INT). A show with a small cast and minimum scenic requirements, and scored for piano or small combo accompaniment.

Little-known but worth producing (LK). A musical that is not famous but that offers excitement and challenge to the amateur producer.

We offer one other precaution to keep in mind when selecting a musical: Do not confuse film versions of musicals with their stage counterparts. While some film versions are faithful to the original stage shows (*My Fair Lady*, for example), many others are changed substantially in the transfer from stage to screen. Songs, characters, and dance numbers may be added, dropped, or altered, and even the plot itself may be vitally changed. Stage versions of plays such as *Cabaret, Grease, On a Clear Day You Can See Forever, The Unsinkable Molly Brown,* and *Paint Your Wagon* underwent many changes when they were converted to motion pictures. A producer is well advised to read a stage version of a musical before making a decision to go ahead with production plans.

CASTING THE MUSICAL

When a musical is being cast, the most immediate problem is *who* is to do the casting. If a director is working with a choreographer and a music director or vocal coach, each of these three people may lobby strongly for performers who specialize in his or her area. It has long been a cliché in the theatre that singers can't dance, dancers can't sing, and actors can't do either. Fortunately, most modern musicals do not require that performers step beyond their areas of special talent to any great extent, although the actors, singers, and dancers are not now as compartmentalized as they were in early musicals. Nevertheless, it is imperative to remember that the director is the individual faced with the problem of projecting the whole and unified production to an audience. Even before casting, therefore, it should be established that the director's final word is law.

There are certain problems that can arise when a music director is allowed to handle casting. A case in point is a production of *Carousel* that was cast by the music department of the sponsoring institution. They chose a very fine actor and wonderful singer to play Billy Bigelow, the leading male role, but this actor was only 5′4″. That meant that most of the other characters

Figure 3. Scene from *The Drunkard; or, The Fall'n Saved.* In the Colby-Sawyer College production, an all-women cast appeared in the stylized production of the old melodrama. Period songs were used within the action and as interludes. Directed and designed by Hope Fitzgerald; scripted by Haller Laughlin. Photograph by Haller Laughlin.

had to be smaller than he, and he had to be specially placed in chorus numbers to suggest greater height. He was able to both play and sing the role, but, even though he was an actor who had worked in many nonmusical productions, he was not a person that a director with experience and production overview would have chosen to play Billy. Physically he was not the best choice for the part. Consequently, if the director—who knows the problems of the whole show in relation to sets, audiences, costumes, and interrelations with other characters—is assigned the task of casting, he or she will, of course, consult with co-staff members, but it should be this director who has the last word about casting.

There are five preaudition tactics the director can use to aid the cause. First, the director can select an assistant director, in advance, to help in conducting the auditions. A well-trained helper is invaluable for directing traffic, issuing instructions, and following up on any ideas that may occur to the director during the casting sessions. Second, the director can advertise scenes and songs to be used in the auditions and make scripts available well in advance for perusal by interested performers. Third, the director can be sure records or tapes of the musical numbers to be used in the auditions are available at a public center, such as a library; however, these scripts, tapes, or records should be used on the premises and not removed, so that anyone interested in them can have access to them. Fourth, the director can advertise that only music from the show being produced will be used at the auditions. Otherwise, when allowed to select their own music, singers will often choose songs and keys that fit nicely into their own range but that may vary considerably in style or musical structure from the music in the show being done.

Finally, the director can use the preparatory tactic of providing forms at auditions for prospective performers and crew members to fill out. (See Figures 4 and 5.) These forms provide valuable information which can be easily organized and immediately used, or filed for further use. Two sample forms that may be used or adapted are offered here.

Many directors prefer to conduct reading auditions for a musical in the same manner as for a nonmusical. In such cases, separate singing and dancing auditions are held. Still other directors prefer a different audition procedure that allows for more individual contact with the auditionee.

One effective way for the director to conduct the casting for a musical is to read the scenes or speeches with the prospective performers in private, on a one-to-one basis. This method gives the director an opportunity of talking with the performers and getting an initial impression of their personalities. Personalities are especially important in a musical, where roles sometimes lacking in dimension must be fleshed out by the charisma of the performer.

At the same time, the musical director can be conducting singing auditions, and the choreographer, in another location, can be conducting dance auditions. If space is limited, locate an office for the reading, a stage

Figure 4. Audition Form

PLEASE PRINT

NAME_____AGE_____HEIGHT_____
    (LAST)   (FIRST)

ADDRESS_____PHONE_____

SCHOOL_____(CLASS)_____

SCHOLASTIC AVERAGE_____MAJOR_____MINOR_____

MEMBERSHIP IN OTHER ORGANIZATIONS_____

_____

DO YOU SING?_____DANCE?_____

MUSICAL INSTRUMENTS PLAYED_____

WORK PREFERENCE (CITE TWO, E.G., ACTING, PROPS)

1._____

2._____

LIST PREVIOUS EXPERIENCE PERFORMING AND IN TECHNICAL DUTIES ON REAR OF SHEET.
CITE LOCATION AND GROUP IN WHICH YOU WORKED.

YOUR DAILY SCHEDULE (INCLUDE ANY CONFLICTS, RECURRING OR OCCASIONAL)

TIME	MON.	TUES.	WED.	THUR.	FRI.	SAT.	SUN.
3 - 4							
4 - 5							
5 - 6							
6 - 7							
7 - 8							
8 - 9							
9 - 10							
10 - 11							

IS THERE A PARTICULAR ROLE FOR WHICH YOU WISH TO BE CONSIDERED?_____

IF SO, WHICH?_____

WILL YOU ACCEPT ANY ROLE?_____

Figure 5. Production Crew Application

IF YOU WOULD LIKE TO WORK ON ONE (OR MORE) CREWS TO HELP MOUNT A SHOW, AND/OR
IF YOU HAVE A PREFERENCE AS TO WORK AREA, CREW HEAD, CREW MEMBERS, ETC.,
PLEASE USE THIS FORM TO HELP US MAKE CREWS ASSIGNMENTS.

IF YOU HAVE NOT HEARD FROM US BY A WEEK OR SO AFTER AUDITIONS FOR A SHOW,
PLEASE CONTACT US AGAIN. SOME CREWS SUCH AS LIGHTS, COSTUMES, MAKE-UP, AND
PAINT DO NOT START WORK RIGHT AWAY, WHILE OTHERS DO. WE DO WANT TO USE YOU,
BUT SOMETIMES A NAME OR REQUEST GETS LOST UNINTENTIONALLY.

PLEASE WATCH THE PRODUCTION CALL BOARD FOR CREW MEETINGS, WORK CALLS AND OTHER
ANNOUNCEMENTS. CHECK THE CALL BOARD DAILY WHILE INVOLVED IN A SHOW.

NAME_____ PHONE_____

ADDRESS_____

PRODUCTION APPLYING FOR_____

JOB	CREW MEMBER	CREW HEAD	EITHER
SET CONSTRUCTION			
SCENE PAINTING			
PROP GATHERING			
PROP CONSTRUCTION			
LIGHTING HANG			
LIGHT BOARD			
SHIFT CREW			
COSTUMES			
MAKE-UP			
STAGE MANAGER			

for the singing, and some corridor area for the dancing. The musical director will then accompany the singers or will work with an accompanist, and the choreographer can use a tape recording of the music with a portable tape player. Before the audition session, however, the musical director should record a tape of the score with piano accompaniment—both as it is written and at a slower, rehearsal tempo. These recordings will be a great help to the choreographer. Too many people begin casting and rehearsing with an original cast album, only to discover later that whole sections of musical numbers that appear in the score were omitted from the album. This is particularly true of dance segments, which are rarely included on cast albums. The choreographer should audition the aspirants both individually and in small groups of five or six to see how well they follow patterns and work with each other. If solo or duo dance work is called for, a different session might be needed to audition the more accomplished dancers.

Following each of several sessions of this kind of casting, the director, music director, and choreographer should convene to discuss their lists and determine who is absolutely impossible in any category. Of course, if there are aspirants who are impossible in all categories, they are simply eliminated from a callback session. But someone who can act but cannot dance or sing, may be cast, for there are still roles in most productions that require acting only (for example, Flo Ziegfeld in *Funny Girl* or Howard, the producer, in *Applause*). The same holds true for dancers who cannot sing or singers who cannot dance. Don't eliminate people because they cannot do all three things. There is often the necessity of filling the stage for crowd scenes, for example, and people who cannot sing may help accomplish this. Those who sing only slightly can also add to the vocal volume required by many large production numbers. Shows that can accommodate large choruses can be highly successful at the box office and equally helpful in promoting the producing organization's service to the community or educational institution. Just remember that the larger the cast, the more advance planning is needed so as to avoid wasting cast members' time or, worse, total chaos.

Callback sessions need careful thought. They should always begin with physical and vocal warm-ups. In addition to having people read scenes from the musical at a callback session, the director may include a short dialogue sequence and have auditionees memorize *both* parts so that the director can mix performers in different combinations. We suggest the following exercise as a workable possibility for this kind of audition technique.

Callback Exercises

One: Hi!
Two: Hi!
One: Uh—

Two: Uh, what?
One: Uh—how's everything?
Two: The same.
One: I'm surprised to see you here.
Two: I'm surprised to see you here, too.
One: Are you doing anything for a while?
Two: No, not much.
One: Can we do something together?
Two: For a little bit, sure.
One: Swell.
Two: Swell.

This exercise is valuable because its lack of specificity allows the director to assign auditionees characters that depend on movement, such as melting snowmen, two people caught in one panel of a revolving door, atoms in space, mechanical toys, frogs, ducks, kangaroos, and so forth. Also, the exercise tests the performers' ability to maintain a rhythmic delivery of lines while adjusting their delivery to the movements of their bodies. As well, it allows the director to detect a sense of teamwork that would not be observable if the actors were simply standing onstage reading lines from scripts.

It is possible, also, to carry over this idea to aid the choreographer and music director. For example, the director might suggest to a couple that the dialogue is between members of a chorus line, Charlestoners in the Roaring Twenties, or Indians dancing around a bonfire. To others it might be suggested that the dialogue is a recitative from an opera or a toothpaste commercial for television. The dialogue could be material for country/western singers, punk rock singers, or singers of some other distinctive styles of music. In this casting situation performers will loosen up very quickly, and playing to each other will cause whole aspects of personalities to emerge that might not have done so under more stifling conditions.

Once the director has completed this exercise, it is a good idea to use some group pantomimes with the actors, dividing the auditionees into groups of five or six and interchanging them among the assigned roles in pantomimes in which concentration is solely on the body. We offer the following suggestions for group pantomime situations. In all cases it is desirable that the director attempt to adapt the situations of the pantomimes to the types of character relationships found in the musical being produced.

Pantomime Exercises

1. A group of young people are playing basketball when the new kid on the block suddenly appears.
2. A group of executives vie for the attention of a new, attractive secretary during a board meeting.

3. Several badly sunburned individuals attend a social gathering and painfully pretend to be having a good time.

4. At a pajama party a young girl suddenly chokes on a pretzel, and her friends attempt all types of ludicrous remedies.

5. A group of small children accidentally break a valuable lamp and try to destroy the evidence.

6. A group of people riding on top of an open air bus are caught in a rainstorm.

7. A group of people in a crowded elevator become stranded in the dark between floors.

8. A group of people in the presence of a rock star are determined to go home with the souvenir of a lifetime.

Following this, it is a good idea for the director to march all the auditionees in unison, giving them some type of complex march routine. We find this is preferable to having them repeat dance patterns unless the script demands a certain dance technique, such as tap dancing. It is also possible for the musical director to offer some type of marching song to be used during the march. This will help keep the overall group in musical unison as the subgroups split and march in different directions. The following examples of movement patterns may also be used as a part of dance callbacks.

Dance Audition Steps

Circle walk. Have auditionees walk in a circle in time to either taped music from the show or a record of popular music. Have everyone start on the same foot and see who has a sense of rhythm and who can stay on the correct foot. Repeat, using a slow run.

Basic Charleston step. Have auditionees stand in rows, facing the choreographer, who can then explain and demonstrate this step. Stand with feet together. Step forward with right foot (1), kick left foot (2), step back with left foot (3), and touch right toe behind left foot (4) in this pattern:

               2 Left kick
           3 Left   1 Right
           4 Right toe back

Extend the right arm in front of the body with the left kick. Reverse the step beginning on the left foot.

Simple cross-step combination. Have auditionees stand in rows across stage with feet together. Step right, cross left in front of right, step right, cross left in front of right, kick right, step right and reverse, starting with the left foot. Then, slide together four times to the right and reverse. Arms should be out to the side on the slides.

Use these steps with three different floor patterns (circular, backward and forward, side to side). The movement patterns may not all work as well for the same music. The choreographer should, of course, practice the steps in advance with the music selected for the auditions to determine which music works best with which pattern.

Cakewalk kicks (as an alternative or just a "fun" thing). Have auditionees stand close together in a line with feet together. Step right, kick left leg low across the right leg; Step left, kick right leg low across the left leg. Repeat in time to the music. Arms should be to the side while the head turns in the direction of the foot on which one is standing. When done slowly, these kicks will show who has good balance and body control.

Callback sessions for a musical should continue for two hours or more. This extended time is the only way to determine if actors will be able to sustain the energy output level that musical rehearsals will require of them. Throughout the callbacks, the director must keep in mind that the purpose is to acquire a cast of people who will work well together. No matter how brilliant a singer or dancer a performer may be, if the performer shows little ability to work well with others in an audition setting, by giving of herself or himself, enjoying what others are doing, or being helpful to others, then do not use that performer in your musical. A musical involves too many people in too many tense situations, small backstage areas, and crowded dressing rooms to allow personality conflicts. Sooner or later, the person who is not really a team player will cause negative results in the actual show during performances. This is particularly true with inexperienced people. Despite their attempts to hide it, their attitudes toward other performers will be evident onstage.

At the same time that they are searching for talent, looks, charm, and ability to work well in a group, the director, choreographer, and music director must try to relax the auditionees and minimize tension. Auditioning for any play can be an agonizing experience, and musicals tend to compound this problem with their additional requirements for singing and dancing. In a musical, especially one with a large cast, it is imperative that everyone enjoy the experience. If they do not, they will be unlikely to return for future involvement, and the show itself can turn into a debacle, driving the director back to small-cast nonmusicals forever. Once again, let us stress that the greatest enjoyment by cast, crew, and staff will come from a well-organized production headed by a director firmly in control.

It is helpful to remember that one of the basic reasons for callbacks is to give the director, choreographer, and music director a chance to concentrate their attention on fewer people. It is not necessary to call back everyone a director intends to use in the production. One of the emphases at callbacks for musicals is on the casting of the *principal* speaking, singing, and dancing roles.

Following a staff meeting, after the callback session, the director should be ready to have the stage manager post the cast, with the clear knowledge that much careful thought has been put into the selection. A wise director, nonetheless, appoints understudies on the casting list, usually people cast in smaller chorus or one-scene roles, and puts them in observation positions from the very first rehearsal. Forethought is the key to performance safety in this case.

DIRECTING THE MUSICAL

In the planning stages for a musical, the director should be aware of certain structural aspects of the genre. Scenes in a musical are usually written in an economical fashion. Quite often a scene will not climax in dialogue as it does in a nonmusical. Rather, it will climax in a song or a dance. In this case the song or dance not only is the climax of the scene but also serves as the energy highpoint of the scene. Therefore, the director must make sure that the choreographer, if one is used, understands that the dances must extend the characterizations and the stylistic/imagistic concepts of the show as well as move the plot forward. For this reason it is far better for the director, who has the most complete grasp of the show as a whole, to stage the solo musical numbers or those performed by few characters, as well as to block the movement for the nonmusical segments of the show.

Musicals utilize two different forms of stage movement: blocking and choreography. Even within a single musical number, one usually finds it necessary to use both of these forms. Blocking is the movement assigned to the actors. It strengthens the characters and underscores the importance of the dialogue. It places actors in compositions that make interesting stage pictures, allowing the audience to focus on the characters and situations intended by the director. Musical dance sections, conversely, are choreographed, as they are determined by rhythm, tempo, and dynamic markings in the musical score. Choreography refers to dances created by assigning individual steps to performers to use during each musical number. A potential problem exists if choreographers stage musical numbers by resorting to familiar dance steps rather than by employing movement patterns that extend the character and the action.

It is the director's responsibility to make sure that the actors, singers, and dancers are capable of extending their characters from the nonmusical sections of dialogue through the lyrics, melodies, and dances that continue and expand the characters in the show. As we have already pointed out, musicals have often been written for specific personalities more than for performers. Consequently, shows like *The Music Man*, *Funny Girl*, and *Hello, Dolly!* can take on different auras depending upon the personalities of the performers cast in the key roles. When dealing with amateur performers without strongly projected personalities, the director may encounter problems in making the musical show come to life fully for the audience. For example, one need only look at the shows written to star Ethel Merman (*Happy Hunting, Anything Goes, Call Me Madam, Annie Get Your Gun, Gypsy*) to see that the personal qualities necessary for her character's audience relationship are not all written into the dialogue. *Anything Goes* is a big favorite in summer stock companies, but without a strong personality in the Reno Sweeney role, the show is in trouble. And who would dare do *Gypsy* without a strong personality in the role of Rose?

In planning, the director needs to consider the play in small pieces. Just as in nonmusicals, each character has a superobjective, which is the one thing the character must accomplish to aid the show to its logical finish. In addition, each character has an objective in each scene, which is a subdivision of the superobjective. For example, in *Gypsy*, Rose's superobjective is to make a star of her daughter. As the play progresses she achieves the following objectives: She enters her daughter in talent contests, she creates a vaudeville act for her daughter, she pawns family treasures to obtain costumes, she entertains producers who can further her daughter's career, and so forth. She achieves her superobjective: her daughter becomes a star—but, ironically, it is not the daughter she anticipated. The director must take time to explain to all actors, including chorus members, how they are contributing to the enhancement of all these parts of the show. The contributions can be reactions to lines, or exact movement on certain lines, in order to emphasize points or otherwise make the desired impressions of plot on the audience.

Musicals are usually broken into short scenes, and sometimes audiences find it difficult to keep track of all the characters. The characters may appear once and then not be seen again for half an hour, at which time they may bound back onto the stage only to find the audience has forgotten who they are. To help ensure the actors' correct focus on the various characters, the director should compile a character and scene breakdown sheet so that it is clear when, where, and how often each character appears. Two sample breakdowns are included here to illustrate two formats that should be distributed to all cast members.

Character and Scene Breakdown for Small-Cast Musical:
List of Scenes According to Character for
Half a Sixpence

Shop Boys: Scenes Ii, Iii, Iiii, Iiv, Iv, Ivii, Iviii, Ix, IIiii, IIv, IIvi, IIvii, IIviii

Shop Girls: Scenes Ii, Iiii, Ivii, Iviii, IIiii, IIvi

Customers: Scenes Ii, Iiv, Iviii, Iix, Ix

Students: Scenes Ivi, Ivii, Iviii, Iix, Ix, IIviii

Guests: Scenes Ix, IIi, IIvi

Kipps: Every scene except IIvii

Carshot: Scenes Ii, Iii, Iiii, Ivii

Shalford: Scenes Ii, Iii, Iiii, Ivii, IIiii

Mrs. Walsingham: Scenes Ii, Iiii, Iviii, Ix, IIi, IIvi

Mrs. Botting: Scenes Ii, Ix, IIi, IIvi

Ann: Scenes Iii, Ix, IIi, IIii, IIiii, IIiv, IIvi

Helen: Scenes Iiii, Ivi, Iviii, Iix, Ix, IIi, IIvi

Young Walsingham: Scenes Iiii, Iv, Iviii, Ix, IIi

Chitterlow: Scenes Iiii, Iiv, Iv, Ivii

Laura: Scene Iiv

Edith: Scene Ivi

Bert: Scene Ivi

Photographer: Scene IIiii

First Reporter: Scene IIiii

Gwendolyn: Scene IIiv

Character and Scene Breakdown for Large-Cast Musical: List of Scenes According to Character for *Carousel*

	Women	Men	Chorus
Ii	Entire Cast		
Iii	Carrie Julie Mrs. Mullin	Billy 1st Policeman Mr. Bascombe	
Iiii	Carrie Arminy Penny Virginia Susan Nettie Julie Mrs. Mullin	Mr. Snow Billy Jigger	Adult Chorus Children's Chorus Dance Chorus and Captains
IIi	Julie Nettie Carrie	Billy Mr. Snow Jigger	Adult Chorus Children's Chorus
IIii	Julie Nettie Carrie	Jigger Mr. Snow Bascombe	Adult Chorus Children's Chorus

		Mrs. Mullin	Sailor	
				1st Policeman
				2nd Policeman
				Captain
				Heavenly Friend
IIiii			Starkeeper	
			Billy	
			Heavenly Friend	
IIiv	Louise		Mr. Snow	Ruffian Boys
	Jennie			Snow Children
				Dance Chorus
				Solo Dancer
IIv	Carrie		Billy	
	Julie		Heavenly Friend	
	Louise		Mr. Snow	
			Enoch, Jr.	
IIvi	Julie		Dr. Seldon	Adult Chorus
	Nettie		Mr. Bascombe	Children's Chorus
	Carrie		Mr. Snow	
	Louise		Principal	
			Billy	
			Heavenly Friend	

A director must also remember that musicals should progress at a rapid rate. Singers and dancers often beg a director to slow the tempo of a number so that their jobs will be easier, but the minute the numbers are slowed, they lose their original vitality. It is the energy emanating from the stage that sweeps an audience into an emotional relationship with the show. A recently viewed college production of an operetta ran three hours and twenty minutes with two ten-minute intermissions. The tempo of the musical numbers was so slow that it tended to lull the audience to sleep. Nor did the show need all the reprises that were included. A director should leave an audience wanting more. It is much better to have people go backstage saying, "Oh, we would have loved for you to repeat that number." The director can always invite them to return the next evening.

The actors in a musical share a much more direct relationship with their audience than they would in a realistic, nonmusical play. The audience for a musical never has the feeling of looking through a fourth wall at continuing action; therefore, the director and actors must concentrate on creating the proper relationship with the audience through the extension of the actors' personalities across the footlights. The actors need to be able to involve the audience in a kind of theatrical conspiracy, deliberately enticing the audience members to share moments with them. The director must there-fore be on constant guard to keep the actors from playing to each other to the extent that they exclude the house. This is not to suggest that, during musical numbers, actors should be lined up down center, staring directly into the faces of the audience, but body angles and stage positions should be kept open to allow the actors freedom to turn and relate to the audience whenever necessary.

If necessary, the director must take time to explain to the musical director and choreographer the closeness of the relationship between the audience and the singers and dancers. An old theatre adage states that, in scenes involving the chorus, lines of dialogue should be given to dancers rather than singers because the dancers, with their involvement in the rhythmic patterns of the show, have a better concept of "moving the show along." It may be difficult for the director to convince the vocal coach and the musical director that the audience will care much less about the quality of the singers' voices than about their ability to project personalities and enthusiasm, but it is nonetheless true. Broadway's history is filled with examples of this. Debbie Reynolds does not claim to be a trained singer, and yet she played to sold-out houses for a year in *Irene* because of her ability to establish instant rapport with her audience. Rex Harrison in *My Fair Lady*, Richard Burton in *Camelot*, Tammy Grimes in *The Unsinkable Molly Brown*, and Robert Preston in *The Music Man* relied much less on singing ability than on acting skill and the ability to charm audiences into believing in their characters, thereby turning each characterization into a tremen-dously successful portrayal.

During the prerehearsal planning period for a musical, the director must be aware of the following points. It might be helpful to make them into a checklist.

1. The director must know the audience in question and examine the play script carefully to make sure the themes and plot are both in-teresting and acceptable to the audience. The director must also be able to identify a suitable protagonist, who is the one character for whom the audience should have full sympathy. Occasionally a musical will appear in which no character elicits sympathy. *Bajour* and *Pacific Overtures* are two that offer problems in this area, and it becomes increasingly difficult to maintain audience involvement in these shows. The director must decide which characters are being emphasized in the production. The character with whom the audi-ence sympathizes most may or may not be the central character. For example, Billy Bigelow is the central character in *Carousel*, but the director may decide that the audience's sympathy will lie more with Julie, his wife, and may accordingly decide to emphasize the sympathetic aspects of this character.

2. The director must examine available talent to determine if sufficient acting, singing, and dancing ability are at hand. If not, and a particular show must be done, the director must divine the best possible method to utilize the talent which is available.

3. The director must analyze the existing stage facilities in terms of the requirements of the show.

4. The director must consider the experience and skill of the assistants. To what extent must the work of the designers, technical director, musical director, or choreographer be supplemented?

5. The director must break the show down into small sections so that rehearsals can be conducted with certain groups on certain nights. Thus, a minimum amount of time will be wasted in rehearsals. Everyone will work during each rehearsal that he or she attends, and no one will have to wait around for hours for a special scene to come up. Fortunately, most musicals are already divided into short scenes, but a director may want to divide the script further into "French scenes," the beginnings and endings of which are determined by the entrances and exits of selected characters. This is especially helpful with choruses, as their rehearsals can be held at the same times each week. Included here are two examples of how a musical can be broken down into, and rehearsed in, French scenes.

Sample French Scene Division—Ensemble Musical: *The Boy Friend*

Act I

Scene	Pages	Characters
i	1-2	Hortense & girls
ii	2-3	Polly, girls & boys
iii	3-6	Girls, Polly, Madame
iv	6-8	Bobby, Maisie
v	8-9	Hortense, Percival, Madame
vi	9-12	Girls, Polly
vii	12-13	Ensemble—Tony

Act II

i	14-15	Boys & girls
ii	15-16	Lord & Lady Brockhurst, boys & girls
iii	16-18	Girls, Polly, Tony
iv	18-19	Polly, Tony, Hortense
v	19-21	Hortense, boys & girls
vi	21-23	Percival, Madame, Lord & Lady Brockhurst

Scene	Pages	Characters
vii	23-25	Percival, Madame, girls
viii	25-27	Maisie, boys
ix	27-28	Tony, Polly
x	28-30	Full cast

Act III

Scene	Pages	Characters
i	31-32	Hortense, Waiter, chorus, Lord Brockhurst, Madame, Percival
ii	32-33	Madame & Percy
iii	33-36	Bobby, Maisie, chorus
iv	36	Tony, Hortense
v	36-38	Lord Brockhurst, Dulcy, chorus
vi	38-40	Full cast (no Hortense or Tony)
vii	40-42	Full cast
viii	42-44	Full cast

Sample French Scene Division — Musical with Chorus:
Half a Sixpence

Act I

Scene	Pages	Characters
Ii	1-5	Shop boys, girls, Carshot, Shalford, Kipps, Helen, Mrs. Walsingham, Mrs. Botting
Ii	5-6	Shop ballet (dancers), shop workers
Iii	6-13	Shop boys, Kipps, Carshot, Shalford, Ann, extras
Iiii	13-20	Mrs. Walsingham, Helen, shop workers, Chitterlow
Iiiia	20-21	Extras, Chitterlow, Kipps
Iiv	21-25	Laura, Chitterlow, Kipps, shop boys, extras
Iv	25-26	Chitterlow, Kipps, extras, Shalford, Walsingham
Ivi	26-31	Students, Helen, Kipps, Shalford
Ivii	33-37	Shop staff, Chitterlow
Iviii	37-44	Shop workers, Helen, Walsingham, Mrs. Walsingham
Iix	44-47	Company, Helen, Kipps
Ix	48-54	Shop workers, Walsingham, Helen, Kipps, Mrs. Bottins, Mrs. Walsingham, Ann

Act II

Scene	Pages	Characters
IIi	57-61	Society group, Kipps, Ann
IIii	61-64	Ann, Kipps

6. Long before rehearsals begin, months before if possible, the director should sit down with the script and read it through non-stop several times in order to examine the dialogue and locate lines that might be offensive, unclear, or archaic. Unclear lines or references in the script can often be dealt with through the style of the actor's performance or through some visual means in the setting, costumes, or properties. At this time, the director should consider the possibility of deleting any extraneous material connected with the show or any stage business that is beyond the abilities of the performers.

7. The director must conduct an in-depth analysis of the characters in the play. This will aid in casting and also later in rehearsals in helping the actors develop their roles.

8. The director must pay careful attention to the exposition of the script—those lines, lyrics, or business that explain to the audience the developing plot—and to any lines that may explain important character relationships. In *Carousel* there is an interesting blooper involving the character of Mr. Snow. In an early scene in the show, his fiancée, Carrie Pipperidge, introduces him to other characters, who are overjoyed to meet him finally. Later, Mr. Snow is excused from clean-up detail at a community clambake because he won the treasure hunt the previous year—when, indeed, he has only arrived in the community that same day. In a careful analysis, a director would discover and deal with such a mistake.

9. The director should do as much outside reading as possible concerning not only the playwright, composer, and lyricist, but also comments about the show and its characters. In addition, critical commentary about previous productions of the play may prove helpful.

10. The director must work with the various designers to prepare the technical plots (such as lighting and scenery) so that crews may begin work as early as possible, and the designers will be able to clarify what is needed of each crew.

11. Using the designer's floor plan, the director must plan the entrances, exits, and traffic patterns of the characters. Of particu-

lar importance is any change in floor level that the director can use in blocking scenes and staging musical numbers. A change of elevation can be used to achieve proper balance and focus in the stage composition, while at the same time giving the audience an interesting stage picture to watch. The choreographer also should study the elevations to see how the various levels can be used in dance numbers.

12. The director should consult with the costumer to determine the number and types of costumes needed, and to discuss how the costumes can provide extensions of the character's personalities as set out by the playwright and interpreted by the director. For example, in *West Side Story* it is important that the audience always be able to distinguish the Jets from the Sharks, two teen-age gangs involved in street warfare. In the original production, the Sharks were kept in blues and purples and the Jets in oranges and yellows. In the midst of this bevy of colors, the heroine was dressed in white to make her stand out from the crowd.

13. The director must prepare a detailed property plot, listing all set, hand, and wet properties that will be needed in the show. Properties should be listed by scene, location on the setting, and by the actor(s) using them.

14. The director or the appropriate designer must do makeup drawings and diagrams as soon as the show is cast. (See Figure 9 for makeup chart.)

15. The director must determine and provide for any sound cue not provided by the orchestra.

16. The director should consult with the lighting designer to determine the amount and type of light required to carry out the images of the production. Focus, mood, intensity, and cues should all be determined.

17. The director must be able to translate the play script into visual sequences. Moving toy figures or board-game tokens on a scale model or an enlarged floor plan may be helpful. The use of such tokens can be especially beneficial to the novice director who needs help in keeping the locations of various characters clearly in mind. The sequences of movement are then placed into the master script so that during blocking rehearsals they can easily be passed on to the actors. A huge potential problem in musical rehearsal is having actors, singers, and dancers waiting while a director or a choreographer tries to figure out what comes next. This can easily be avoided with some careful prerehearsal planning and blocking.

18. After all of the preceding preparations have been made, the

director should construct a rehearsal schedule that shows the times, the scheduled scenes, the actors needed for each rehearsal, and the approximate duration of the rehearsals. The director should be prompt in beginning and ending rehearsals according to the schedule.

19. In casting the play, the director must look for vocal and physical talent, personality, and also the intelligence, maturity, sensitivity, and temperament for teamwork that are so necessary in compiling a good musical production.

Concerning the matter of blocking, the director may wish to reproduce and distribute sheets with blocking symbols and descriptions, such as the one listed below. These shortcut symbols save a great deal of rehearsal time and provide the actors with a written record of what the director expects of them. A beginning director would do well to remind inexperienced actors often during the blocking rehearsals to write down their blocking. Blocking is often not remembered unless it is written in the script so it can be memorized as lines are memorized.

Blocking Notations

X	cross (move from position to position on stage)
T	turn
S	stand
ST	sit
R	right
C	center
L	left
D	downstage (toward audience)
U	upstage (away from audience)
3/4	45-degree angled position as opposed to profile position
tbl	table
ch	chair
sfa	sofa
stl	stool
bn	bench

Additional furniture can be indicated by similar abbreviations. Also, when there is more than one chair, sofa, or table, they can be differentiated by identifying them as Rch or Lsfa, or numbering them as ch1 or stl5.

Sample Directions

XDR	cross down right
T3/4UL	turn three-quarters up left

STLch	sit left chair
SXRC	stand and cross right center
XDLC	cross down left center
Xch1	cross [to] chair 1
XURsfa	cross up right [to] sofa

With a musical, for which the scripts are often rented, and from which scripts all marks must be erased, these symbols prove doubly effective. The director's master script should include not only the blocking for all the characters but also a floor plan ready for immediate reference (see Figure 6), a copy of the rehearsal schedule, a directory of all cast members with their home addresses and telephone numbers, a properties list, and a cue sheet for sound and light cues (in addition to having them indicated in different colors throughout the script at proper points). As an example of how blocking, staging, and motivation should be indicated, we offer the following section of such a master script from a production of *Melissa and the Magic Nutcracker*, a musical fantasy for children, with book and lyrics by Joseph Robinette, from a short story by Haller Laughlin, music by Karl Jurman. The scene, early in the action, must centralize characters for important exposition. The aged characters must do a brief dance (staged by a director) to a music-box type of tune. These old-fashioned dance steps establish the characters' age and contribute to the nonrealistic style of the production. As a children's show, the musical should have even more movement than a standard musical in order to keep the young audience's attention. Franklin's entrance is attended by a light modification: he will later appear in another guise and must not be clearly seen at this moment.

Figure 6. Stage Floor Plan

UR	UC	UL
RC	C	LC
DR	DC	DL

AUDIENCE

Excerpt with Blocking from the Master Script for
Melissa and the Magic Nutcracker

JESSIMINE

at window UC

Oh, why did our dear daughter, Jennifer, have to move away in the first place?

JEREMIAH

x to her, hands on shoulders

Because she married Monroe Montgomery who just happened to live in Georgia.

JESSIMINE

Why couldn't he have moved up here?   *T to him*

JEREMIAH

Because of the plantation. He couldn't very well have

hug her

raised cotton in Bar Harbor, Maine.

(Pause)

hold her away

Course I probably could've made a sailor out of him.

JESSIMINE

No thank you. One in the family is quite enough.

Sometimes too much, I'm thinking.   *tweaks his nose*

(They laugh)   *she x to fireplace;*
adjust wreath

JEREMIAH

Grandma, Melissa's going to love it here. We'll show her a fine time. Right, Matey?

x to coatrack UL

(*He goes to his coat and looks in the*
pocket. Squeaking noises are heard.)

Sound #2

JESSIMINE

Now, Grandpa, you keep that pet mouse of yours out of sight while Melissa's here.   *turn x 1/2 above sofa & arrange Xmas flowers*

JEREMIAH

Oh, she'll love Matey. We'll tell her all about our sea-going adventures together. Right, Matey?

(*A squeak is heard.*)   *Sound #3*

JESSIMINE

he puts coat back

Just the same, you keep him tucked away.

(Singing)

JESSIMINE

MELISSA
A MOUSE IN THE HOUSE   *x to him, shake finger*
IS NOT WHAT WE WANT
    OUR SWEET LITTLE GRANDCHILD TO SEE!
INSTEAD IN HER BED
A DOLL SHE SHOULD SPY   *x to tree, pick up present*
    AND PRESENTS ALL UNDER THE TREE!

JEREMIAH
(Holding up gifts)
A SPONGE RUBBER BALL,   *x to closet—carry out large*
A WOODEN BIRD CALL,   *pile of packages*
    TO THINK THAT I MADE 'EM MYSELF!
                they counter cross, he to tree, she to kitchen door

JESSIMINE
AND NOW I SHALL BAKE
SOME COOKIES AND CAKE
TO FILL UP MY BIG PANTRY SHELF!

JEREMIAH
                                they come together to minuet
(Chorus)
IT'S ALL FOR MELISSA, MELISSA
    WHO'S COMING FROM SO FAR AWAY!

JESSIMINE
MELISSA, MELISSA,
    ARRIVING ON THIS VERY DAY!
BOTH
AND YEARS FROM NOW WHEN SHE'S   *they allemande to L*
    FULLY GROWN
WE HOPE SHE'LL REMEMBER THIS
    CHRISTMAS AS THE BEST
    SHE'S EVER KNOWN!

JESSIMINE
IS EVERYTHING SET?   *she runs to tree*

JEREMIAH
ALL SET NOW, YOU BET!   *he hornpipes around*
EVERYTHING'S FINE AS CAN BE!   *the room L to R—*
    YOU'VE SCRUBBED THE WHOLE PLACE,   *pointing at*
    INCLUDING MY FACE,   *objects*
NOT ONE SPECK OF DIRT DO I SEE!

JESSIMINE
IS THERE ENOUGH FOOD?   *runs to kitchen door*

JEREMIAH

NOW GRANDMA YOU'VE STEWED AND   *he catches her & they*
CANNED ENOUGH FOOD TO   *dance step back to C*
FEED A WHOLE ARMY OR TWO!
YOU'VE GIVEN YOUR BEST,
NOW TAKE A SHORT REST,
YOU'VE DONE EVERYTHING YOU CAN DO!

dance here in a circle—fast movement & allemande,
ends with a kiss under
(REPEAT CHORUS)   *the mistletoe*
interrupted by
(There is a knock at the door.)
Sound #4

JEREMIAH

Now who in tarnation can that be?

JESSIMINE

Well, who do you *think* it could be?

BOTH

Double take

Melissa!

(They bump into each other trying to
get to the door. Finally, JEREMIAH
opens it.)

JEREMIAH

Melissa!   *Light #2*

(He throws his arms around the figure
standing there. It is FRANKLIN, a
sailor.)

She's awfully big. Must take after her daddy.   *drags C*

JESSIMINE

x to him, pushes him away

Jeremiah, that's not Melissa.

JEREMIAH

backs up

Oh, sorry, young fella.

Melissa and the Magic Nutcracker.
Westport, Conn.: Dramatic Publishing Company, 1983.

It is wise to remember that the director, when directing a production with very inexperienced people, functions not only as coordinator of all stage movement and physical aspects of the show, but also as an acting coach.

This means that he or she assumes the responsibility for the success of each performance in the production; therefore, it may become necessary to fingertip a performance. Fingertipping means giving line readings and exact gestures for actors to copy, as well as holding private consultations with the actors at which they learn to copy minute inflections in line readings. Some directors may feel that this is simply not a job for the director, since it is the actor who is expected to perform, but the overall success of a show nonetheless rests on each actor's *seeming* to give a performance, no matter who initially conceived the interpretation. If inexperienced performers are incapable of realizing a full-blown portrayal on their own, they must be shown how. After all, young dancers on television are often following the movements of an off-camera dance captain who stays a few beats ahead of them. To be skillful at fingertipping, however, the director must understand each character in terms of motivation, subtext (the thoughts behind the character's words), and the style in which the role is to be played. Although fingertipping is a directorial device for use with inexperienced performers, a director should not hesitate to use it subtly with experienced performers, for the ultimate responsibility for all aspects of any production lies with the director.

COSTUMES AND MAKEUP

The ideal costume for a stage musical is well constructed to enable the actor, dancer, or singer to move easily. Since the musical is often stronger than the nonmusical in the energy level it projects, a musical costume should be more vibrant than a nonmusical one. A costume gives the audience a key to the character wearing it, in terms of the character's historical period, emotional outlook, economic and sociological level, and geographical location. It also, as previously mentioned, can be used as a signpost for an audience to identify both character and character relationships through color, line, or some repeated detail.

In preparing for a musical, the director and costume designer must have consultations concerning the style and images the director is using in the approach to the show so that the costumes will share in conveying these elements. One of the costumer's first duties is to draw up a costume plot or master plan of the costumes required for the play being produced. The following items should be indicated on a costume plot: the number of costumes needed, the specific type of garments required, the number of costume changes during the show, and any special requirements of the production. A chart is the simplest method for outlining the costume plot, with columns designated for the act and scene, the character, the actor, the costume, any accessories needed, and notes for any special requirements or indications. A sample costume plot follows.

Figure 7. Scene from *Kiddleywinks!* The Valdosta State College production, directed by Randy Wheeler, emphasized simple costumes and mobile set pieces. Photograph by deRon Coppage.

Sample Costume Plot for *Carousel* (partial)

Act	Character	Actor	Costume	Accessories	Notes
Ii	Billy Bigelow	Rick D'Onofrio	red turtle-neck shirt; checked pants	plaid news-boy cap	platform shoes
	Julie Jordan	Leslie Jones	pink & white gingham dress	matching draw-string purse	pink ribbon in hair
	Carrie Pipperidge	Terri D'Onofrio	green & white gingham dress	straw hat, drawstring purse	

Musical production staff members often assume that, because of the large number of costumes involved, a director will arrange to rent the garments from a costume company. That can be the least efficacious method of costuming a musical, however. For several reasons, building the costumes for a particular production usually is preferable.

Because musicals involve a great deal of movement, it is important for the performers to rehearse in their costumes longer than they might for a nonmusical. Very few organizations can afford the additional rental charges for an extra week's rehearsal. In addition, many rental costumes prove to be unusable when they arrive. They may restrict dance movement by being too tight, too heavy, or ill-fitting. Because of zippers, buttons, or hooks, they may not allow quick costume changes necessitated by the script. All of this can lead to great discomfort for the performers, which can result in their feeling insecure and ceasing to enjoy their performance. This, in turn, can lead to a poor show. Furthermore, to keep the style of the production immediately apparent and the visual image of the production consistent, the costumes should harmonize with the settings and other visual aspects of the show; rented costumes rarely do this.

It is usually far less expensive, both financially and emotionally, to build costumes than to rent them, and the results are usually better. Another advantage in creating costumes is the establishing of a costume supply from which outfits for future productions can be selected. Such costumes would be well made, with colors and designs well coordinated, and of course there would be no rental fee. If one has the personnel capable of proper costume construction, and if there is adequate storage space for the costumes when the show is over, then one certainly has the basic requirements for making costumes.

If, however, some factor prevents the building of costumes, the next location to search should not be someone's attic or basement. Such garments are not likely to be sufficiently strong in color and texture to carry across to the audience. Also, they rarely allow for the amount and type of movement required of musical performers. Odd sizes usually result in ill-fitting costumes, and the overall result will hardly match any director's image of the show.

If and when a director is faced with the need to rent costumes, the first source to try may not be a costume house proper but a college, community theatre, or high school nearby which may have done the same show or perhaps another musical set in the same period. The director may find these costumes to be better made, in a more harmonious blend, and with a much lower rental rate than those to be had from a large, commercial rental house. On top of that, there is likely to be a less-stringent time stricture attached to the rental of these costumes.

Whatever method a director decides upon to obtain costumes for the show, the first rehearsal is the ideal time to measure all actors for costumes. This usually stimulates the actors into an early feeling of direct involvement with the show and a sense of excitement about it. The measurements should be taken by the costumer or a competent member of the costume crew. It is not advisable to ask the actors to write their own measurements. Both men and women are prone to add or subtract a few pounds or inches to make themselves appear more attractive, which results in inaccurate measurements and ill-fitting costumes. Figure 8 presents a good costume measurement form, which can be used for renting or for building costumes. There is more information on this form than will be needed on a rental form, but it is good to keep this information on file. It also offers backup protection in case the rental forms are lost in the mail.

For the director who decides to use a professional costume rental house, Chapter 3 of this book lists, by state, a sampling of several such rental sources. There has been no attempt to include all rental agencies, nor to exclude any for lack of merit. For additional agencies, we suggest that the director consult the *Simon's Directory*, published by Package Publicity Service, 1501 Broadway, Room 1314, New York, New York 10036, (212) 354-1480, which lists not only rental agencies but, also, costume fabric and accessory houses. Most of these costume rental houses will furnish a catalog upon request, listing their offerings. The director should choose a company that is nearby to facilitate selections and substitutions.

Makeup charts should be drawn up in the early stages of production. Figure 9 illustrates a sample makeup chart.

Makeup charts can, in fact, be done as soon as the play has been cast. Makeup can then be ordered, and makeup and hair-dressing sessions can be scheduled outside rehearsal time before dress rehearsals begin. Actors should have time to discuss their makeup designs and application with a makeup crew, if one exists, or with the director. Making up for the show

Figure 8. Costume Measurement Chart

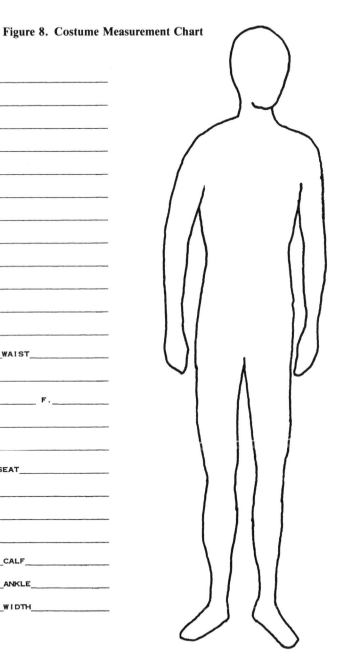

SHOW_____

CHARACTER NAME_____

ACTOR'S NAME_____

PHONE_____

DRESS OR COAT_____

PANTS W. & L._____

SHIRT N. & SL._____

SOCKS & SHOES_____

HAT & HEAD_____

SHOULDERS_____

SH. TO ELB._____

ELB. TO WRIST_____

WRIST_____WAIST_____

NECK_____

NECK TO WAIST B._____ F._____

WAIST TO FLOOR_____

WAIST TO KNEE_____

SITTING: WAIST TO SEAT_____

CHEST OR BUST_____

UNDER BUST_____

UNDER ARMS TO WAIST_____

HIP_____CALF_____

THIGH_____ANKLE_____

FOOT LENGTH_____WIDTH_____

Figure 9. Makeup Chart

PROSTHESIS

PLAY_____

ACTOR_____

CHARACTER_____

AGE_____BASE_____

SHADOWS_____

HIGHLIGHTS_____   CHEEK ROUGE_____

LIP ROUGE_____   EYE SHADOW_____

EYE ACCENTS_____   WRINKLES_____(HI)_____(LO)____

EYEBROWS_____   BODY MAKE-UP_____ON_____

POWDER_____   HAIR COLOR_____

HAIR ARRANGEMENT_____
   (BEARDS, MOUSTACHES, ETC.)

NOTES OR CORRECTIONS

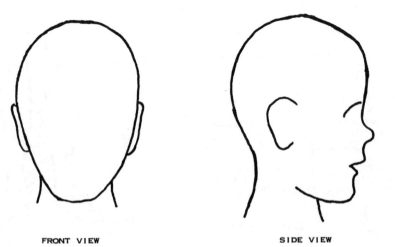

FRONT VIEW   SIDE VIEW

can then become a joy instead of a burden. If there are actors in the cast who are inexperienced in applying makeup, crew members should be assigned to help them. A makeup schedule needs to be arranged so that cast members will not be crowding each other in the dressing rooms. Also, since most musicals have large casts, all unauthorized people should be kept out of the dressing rooms while the actors are applying their makeup. The actors should be kept flowing through the dressing rooms rather than allowed to settle there. A wise additional move is to supply mirrors in some other area, even if it is only a corridor, so that performers can check their costumes and makeup just before making their entrances. They need to learn how to adjust their costumes, as well as how to avoid wrinkling them. A droopy costume can make them appear to be giving a droopy performance. The director and costumer should also caution the actors never to drink, eat, or smoke in costume to avoid unnecessary damage to the garments.

DESIGNING THE SET

As must be obvious by now, producing a musical involves such a tremendous amount of work that choosing a show that the director does not like is unthinkable. But loving the show is not enough. The producing organization must be able to provide the proper scenic backgrounds for the play. The group may choose a play only to be submerged in incredible scenic requirements. *Bye Bye Birdie*, a very popular show with high schools, has seventeen scenes, taking place in fourteen different settings. During the past decade many American colleges have chosen *Cabaret* as their annual musical production. This show calls for an onstage orchestra, eight settings, and a large unlocalized area. Resident and community theatres have found *Mame* to be a popular show with audiences; however, the show calls for a dozen settings, with Mame's famous apartment being redecorated substantially seven times during the performance. Some organizations have the funds, space, and equipment to carry out the scenic requirements as they were executed on Broadway, but these groups are only an enviable minority. So, what does the amateur director with severely limited funds do? First, the director considers the relationship of the setting to the play. A play like *Mame* demands lush and constantly changing settings to reflect the mood of the title character. To curtail the settings drastically will seriously affect the overall effectiveness of the show. Luckily, however, many musicals can have their scenic demands simplified greatly and still remain theatrically intact.

The answer to the question of the scenic demands of a musical lies in what may be referred to as the unit-set system of scene design. In this system, the scene designer meets with both the director and the choreographer, and together they arrive at a single imagistic design for the show. This design must

Figure 10. Scene from *The Music Man*. In the South Georgia College production, directed by Jacqueline Wheeler and with scenes designed by George Hawks and Stephen Hawks, this brief opening scene is played on a rolling platform that can be moved off stage easily, without interrupting the flow of the production. Photograph by Gary Poole.

Figure 11. Scene from *Heritage*. Note the imagistic set and levels and pantomimed props in the Eastern Kentucky University Readers Theatre production of *Heritage*, a series of Civil War journals and letters using period music. Directed and designed by Haller Laughlin. Photograph by Haller Laughlin.

accomplish several tasks. First, it must immediately suggest to an audience the theme of the play and how this theme will be interpreted through the director's overall concept of the production; therefore, the director must come to this planning session with a very clear idea of what the production is to express to an audience. Second, the design must be historically and geographically suggestive; that is, it must suggest the time period and location in which the action is set. Third, the design must meet the needs of the musical performers by enhancing the musical sections of the play and by offering no problems with the singing or choreography.

The imagistic concept of the setting is the all-encompassing design scheme tying the performance elements of time, place, and style together. This can be done most successfully by choosing a visual metaphor that suggests the director's interpretation. Sandy Wilson's *The Boy Friend* serves as an excellent example of how the imagistic concept can be applied to a musical. Three settings are called for in the script. Act I takes place in the salon of Madame Dubonnet in an exclusive girls' school on the French Riviera. Act II takes place on a promenade of the public beach. Act III is set in the courtyard of a cafe during a carnival masked ball. The time period of the play, as stressed by the music and the style of the writing, is the 1920s. The plot is concerned with the love affairs of the various characters.

Since the play deals with love, the theme might well be imagized in a heart motif; the style could be that of a "1920s tab show," a slight show written to tour the provinces and to play in the limited space accorded to those shorter-than-main-stem productions that appeared in the smart supper clubs of London and New York City. Hence, a style of simplified setting begins to take shape—a heart-shaped proscenium arch bordered with lights spelling out the title which can be blinked on and off during musical numbers; a cyclorama with wing pieces; an upstage heart-shaped arch on a platform with several steps leading down. Set changes are thus greatly simplified: curtains hanging on the arch for Act I, a beach sign for Act II, and streamers of lights for Act III. Throughout, the heart shape of the arches can be repeated in the decor, and all set pieces and furnishings can be done in lively shades of blue, white, and pink. Thus, the audience learns immediately from the setting and decor what to expect in terms of the style of the production. This is an immeasurable aid to the cast, and it comes about because the designer and the director have "done their homework" by analyzing the show well in advance. Production costs are lower, set changes are greatly simplified, backstage crews need not be so large, and the show suffers not at all.

Another show in point is a charming musical called *Half a Sixpence*. It is not only excellent for high schools and junior colleges, with its emphasis on a very young cast, but the fact that the last scene takes place in the Christmas season makes it a good preholiday show. *Half a Sixpence* has a variety of turn-of-the-century settings. The action begins in a ribbon-and-dry-goods shop, proceeds to the boardwalk, goes into a local pub, returns to the ribbon shop, and then, in turn, moves to the interior of an art studio, a cabana section of a beach, a chic mansion, a photographer's studio, the foundation of a half-built house, and a little apartment in the rear of a bookstore. All of these constitute a rather large number of sets for a musical that is not particularly well known (no matter how much it is worth producing) and that is not especially geared for a large cast.

The musical has a rags-to-riches theme, with the hero discovering that he was infinitely happier as a poor young man than he is as a wealthy young man, and the dialogue constantly returns to a discussion of his earlier days as a ribbon-and-dry-goods clerk. Hence, all the scene changes and the flow of the show, which is too light in plot and character to bear ornate sets and furnishings, might be easily handled by using an image of an old-fashioned Valentine or Christmas card. This might involve creating a seeming paper-lace frame for the stage, creating the frame and all of the sets out of stylized latticework so that they, too, seem to be cut out of paper lace. Using the dancers—who have two good numbers in the show but otherwise very little to do—as the set changers, and having them "dance" the latticework in and out of various arrangements to form the set pieces for the new scene, would be a good way of avoiding dropping and raising curtains and lengthy scene changes. Audiences who are not very theatrically experienced often grow restless during scene changes, and their attention can easily be lost. This alternate method of scene shifting would enhance their enjoyment of the show by offering them entertainment at a time when they might not expect it.

To expand the imagistic approach, the dancers who serve as the scene changers can be given definite characters, such as dancers or customers in the shop, and can wear their same costumes throughout the show. Other characters in this group might be a couple of elderly ladies, a pickpocket, a fruit seller, an elegant dandy and a young lady with whom he is flirting, a mother with a bevy of daughters of various sizes, and so on. Thus the audience could identify and enjoy these characters each time they saw them. The added surprise of having the latticework appear in various arrangements and designs would result in further audience involvement.

These are only two productions that may be stylized, but with careful analysis an imagistic approach can be taken to many musical and non-musical productions. The director must bear in mind, however, that there are certain shows that will suffer from an imagistic approach. As has already been mentioned, *Mame* needs various scene changes to reflect the leading character's emotional states and current lifestyles. *Man of La Mancha* is another such production. The audience must be constantly aware, as the characters act out for us the story of Don Quixote, that towering above them are guards and executioners, threatening figures from the exterior world of the play. These ominous characters have the ability to abruptly interrupt the flow of action at any moment, thus lending suspense and atmosphere to the production. *Man of La Mancha* is a production that will not work effectively on a stage without height. Certainly one can point out productions like *Zorba* and *Cabaret* as owing much of their Broadway success to the imagistic approach the designer and director took for the style of the productions. The tilted mirror that hovered above the characters throughout all the action of *Cabaret* reflected to the theatre audience a distorted view of themselves, thus making them an integral part of the activity onstage. The tree of life stayed constantly in stage center during *Zorba*, while the platform above the set contained the singers from the cafe in which the tale was being enacted. This made the interpretative characters appear to hover dramatically above the orchestra and to channel sound toward the stage as needed. The designer must keep the audience's sight lines in mind when adding scenery or curtains to mask the backstage areas and should attempt to tie in the masking stylistically to the stage setting.

The director, when analyzing musical scripts for production, becomes aware that often there is extraneous music and, sometimes, extraneous scenes, which were composed for large-scale productions so that they could be played in front of a drop curtain, or traveler, while large sets were being changed behind them. In doing an imagistic production in which the flow of the action is much stronger and fewer sets are required, it is easy to eliminate these scenes, or musical interludes, thus tightening and shortening the show, which will work in the director's and the show's favor when the audience is one that is not theatrically experienced. In addition, this practice will save the cast the wear and tear that would be brought on by having to handle all this material extraneous to the flow of the show.

For audiences who do not attend the theatre regularly, most musicals are too long. Some musicals—*1776*, *Follies*, *Pippin*, and *Man of La Mancha*, for example—do not allow for act breaks. In the original productions, the audience had to remain seated for the entire show. These shows do have areas in the script at which logical breaks in the action can occur, thus allowing for intermissions, which amateur audiences need. The director who selects such a play for production should analyze the construction of the play in advance and find a logical, dramatic point at which the action can be broken and an intermission inserted. In addition, much of the profit from high school, college, and community or resident theatre productions comes from the sale of food and beverages during intermissions. Musicals without intermission breaks therefore cut severely into the profits that are not only expected but needed by those organizations. More importantly, anything a director can do to reduce the overall amount of movement into and out of the theatre during a performance is a decided plus for the production. Many audience members will take a personal intermission when they are not provided one by the director, and in doing so they will interfere with others' enjoyment of the show.

It is imperative that the scene designer provide the director with a floor plan of all settings for the play well before rehearsals begin. This floor plan should clearly indicate any set changes during the action of the play, and it should also indicate any periods in the action at which curtains must be dropped to cover changes. (More information about dealing with this type of situation is found above under the heading "Directing the Musical.") Also, the designer should provide a model or a color rendering of the set so that the director can plan the action of the play on a master script before rehearsals begin. This model, or rendering, can also prove invaluable in early rehearsals by helping the cast envision the set's eventual appearance and size. Blocking will make more sense to the actors then, and they will not be surprised by technical additions when dress rehearsals begin.

The importance of the scene design, in terms of its effect on the director's approach to handling the play script and musical score, must not be underestimated. At least four functions of scene design are readily apparent. First, scene design locates the action of the play in terms of geography (country, climate, indoors, outdoors, and so forth) and time (historical period, season, time of day). Place can also be interpreted to demonstrate the social rank of the characters. Second, scene design establishes a dominant mood for the action and can be seen as a graphic representation of the play's emotional factors. Third, scene design reinforces the theme of the play by giving significance to, and helping to explain, the action in the play. Finally, scene design stages the story. It provides for the flow of the action, either unbroken or with periodic interruptions for changes. It also provides the minimum of physical necessities for the action in terms of entrances, exits, levels, and optimum space. To emphasize further the importance of the role of scene design to the production planning of a musical, we include the following comments by several prominent scene designers.

When the curtain rises, it is the scenery that sets the key of the play. A stage setting is not a background; it is an environment. Players act in a setting, not against it. We say, in the audience, when we look at what the designer has made, before anyone on the stage has time to move or speak, "Aha, I see! It's going to be like that! Aha!"

> Robert Edmond Jones, *The Dramatic Imagination: Reflections and Speculations on the Art of the Theatre.* New York: Theatre Arts Books, 1941, pp. 23-24.

Good designing is good thinking, with freedom of imagination supplanted by reasonable performance in execution.

> Donald Oenslager, *Scenery Then and Now.* New York: W. W. Norton and Company, Inc., 1936, p. xiii.

A good setting is not a picture but an image.

> Mordecai Gorelik, "The Scenic Imagination" (unpublished manuscript).

A good scene . . . is not a picture. It is something seen, but it is something conveyed as well: a feeling, an evocation. . . . It is a presence, a mood, a warm wind fanning the drama to flame. It echoes, it enhances, it animates. It is an expectancy, a foreboding, a tension. It says nothing, but it gives everything.

Jones, p. 26.

As mentioned earlier, the director and scene designer should utilize a fly system for frequent scene shifts if such a system is available in the performance hall. Flying scenery can prevent numerous lags in the rhythm and tempo of the performance, which lessen the show's impact on the audience. If scenery cannot be flown, the next most expedient shifting method is mounting the scenic units on wheels. Heavy-duty casters can be expensive, but they are worthwhile because of the time saved and the smoothness they lend to the scene shift. A word of caution concerning casters: Never scrimp on the budget by buying casters not designed for heavy-duty wear. Scenery can be extremely heavy, and if actors' bodies are added to it, the director needs to ensure maximum safety. Remember, also, to provide adequate backstage storage space for all scenery pieces so that they are accessible when needed and out of the way otherwise.

The lighting design for a musical does not differ significantly from that of a nonmusical except in the use of follow spotlights. For many years it was customary to make extensive use of follow spotlights in musicals. Today, general lighting may be preferable. Very rarely are the productions about which we are writing presented on stages so large that follow spotlights are necessary. Originally these lights were used to differentiate characters when they were singing solos or solo sections of songs while surrounded by large choruses or extravagant settings. Careful directors and designers can arrange choruses and settings so that, even during ensemble scenes, an audience's focus will go to the principal performers without the use of follow spotlights. Moreover, finding crew personnel to operate these spotlights is another burden with which the director can easily dispense.

Follow spotlights may still be called for when scenes in a musical require some type of special effect, such as the lead dancer's dream-sequence number in *Company*, when the rest of the setting should be darkened. Another example might be an opening tableau: For instance, in *The Boy Friend*, using the imagistic approach that we mentioned, it might be interesting to use heart-shaped areas of light (achieved through the use of gobos, extensions on spotlights that give specific shapes to the beam of light). In Act I, the maid's black-hosed leg kicking from the proscenium arch could be spotlighted. In Act II, the characters appear on the beach in a pyramid topped by a beach ball, which also could be spotlighted. In Act III, at the costume ball, a mask carried on a stick could be singled out by light. In such cases, the follow spotlights are not used a great deal, only to carry out the imagistic approach of the director and the designer.

Figure 12. Scene from *Annie Get Your Gun*. In the South Georgia College production directed by Randy Wheeler and with scene design supervised by George Hawks, the second act opens with this scene, set on the deck of a cattle boat. A few well-chosen set pieces and proper ties convey the feeling of the setting without cluttering the stage, while the scene itself can be further isolated by area lighting. Photograph by Glenn Clower.

Whether one needs follow spotlights will also depend on the demands of the orchestra. The conductor may insist on being spotlighted at each appearance in the orchestra area. Also, as previously stated, the physical aspects of the performance hall may require the additional intensity of the follow spotlights. Sometimes, too, individual scenes may require that a specific character be singled out. In *Company*, the central character of Bobby often needs to be separated for solo numbers while other characters are onstage with him. This is an example of the use of follow spotlighting for dramatic advantage, and, as is true with all visual aspects of any production, each element must blend with each other element to result in a unified whole as envisioned by the director's primary image of the show.

PUBLICITY

Another potentially difficult situation arises during rehearsals when the publicity demands are great. The director and cast resent time being taken away from rehearsals to pose for publicity pictures and to give interviews, but this, again, can be avoided through careful planning. A publicity form such as in Figure 13 can be filled out at the first rehearsal by every cast member and given to the publicity director or publicity crew. This will prevent the need for cast and director interviews during the difficult days just before the show opens.

During early rehearsals, a full cast and crew list (never let the crew feel unimportant) should be put together for the local newspapers. Aside from that, all promotion ideas on the production can and should be discussed before rehearsals begin. Try to find a publicity slant that deals with the production as local news, with feature value, rather than relying solely on a plot synopsis and a cast list. For example, a show presented just before Christmas, regardless of whether the plot has anything to do with Christmas, can be advertised as an ideal way to begin the joys of the holiday season. The major characters could even be photographed waving through a wreath. The producing organization should always be aware of the possibility of using holiday or local events to tie in with the show, and should analyze the local papers to see what special columns are available to be used. Even cooking columns can be used to the show's advantage by advertising favorite recipes of the cast. A little imagination and effort early in the schedule can lead to handsome payoffs at the box office.

Early in the rehearsal period a photography session should be set up. Several cast members can be photographed before a suitable background wearing makeup and costume pieces. There is no reason that publicity photographs must wait until the last minute, even though they should look as finished as possible. The director should schedule at least three dress rehearsals, and lobby photographs (posed scenes from the production for lobby display) can be taken at the first of these. At any rehearsal at which

Figure 13. Publicity Form

PLEASE PRINT

NAME_____

CHARACTER PLAYED_____PLAY_____

HOME ADDRESS_____

SCHOOLS ATTENDED_____

PREVIOUS THEATRICAL EXPERIENCE, BRIEFLY_____

_____

_____

_____

IF NON-STUDENT, WORK_____

          CIVIC ORGANIZATIONS_____

IF A STUDENT, SCHOOL ADDRESS_____

        SCHOLASTIC AVERAGE_____CLASS STANDING_____

EXTRA-CURRICULAR ACTIVITIES_____

_____

MAJOR_____

HOMETOWN NEWSPAPERS_____

PARENTS (NAMES, EMPLOYMENT, CIVIC ORGANIZATIONS, ETC.)_____

_____

_____

- -

PRODUCTION DATES_____

PERFORMANCE LOCATION_____

TICKET INFORMATION_____

PLAY SYNOPSIS_____

_____

66

Figure 14. Set from *O, Marry Me.* In the Colby-Sawyer College production, directed and designed by Haller Laughlin, the imagized set concept took advantage of the Thanksgiving season. The simplified seating enhanced the show and the "frame" device allowed for cast enlargement. Photograph by Haller Laughlin.

Figure 15. Scene from *O, Marry Me*. In the show-within-a-show scene, from the Colby-Sawyer College production, directed and designed by Haller Laughlin, the cast played a troupe of eighteenth-century actors performing on a make-shift stage in a barn during a harvest celebration. Photograph by Haller Laughlin.

Figure 16. Publicity Picture for *O, Marry Me*. Since the Colby-Sawyer College production was planned for the Thanksgiving holiday time, the characters were posed early in rehearsal in a harvest wreath. The photograph, released to local newspapers two weeks before opening night, received a good deal of holiday use. Photograph by Haller Laughlin.

photographs are to be taken, the director and stage manager should have an itemized list of the shots, which should begin with the end of the show and move back toward the beginning so that the actors are dressed and the set and properties are ready to begin rehearsal when the photographs have been taken. No matter how complex the production, this session should last no longer than forty minutes. There is no reason to take an inordinate number of photographs. The lobby photographs can also be sent to newspapers as final production prints.

Publicity devices should stress imagination and invention; they are most effective when structured for the local audience. These devices can be divided into two time categories: the early rehearsal period and the performance period. The first category might include inserting promotional flyers into local bank statements and business mailings, newspaper publicity photographs of cast members of the same family, appearances on local television and radio talk shows, distributing photographs with brief publicity captions to complimentary shoppers' guides, placing advertising slides on local television stations, hanging street and mall banners in prominent locations, arranging for local restaurants to create special dishes and desserts named for the production, and distributing table cards to restaurants and school cafeterias. Devices that work best just before and during the actual performances include staging musical numbers at malls, civic clubs, arts festivals, and in parades; cast and crew members wearing T-shirts with a production logo, awarding complimentary tickets at senior citizen luncheons and community centers; inviting local civic groups to usher; and selling show posters and T-shirts in the lobby during intermissions.

Buying prepackaged material from the leasing agency to use in advertising a show can be much less effective than publicity geared to the specific production being presented and the intended audience toward whom the publicity is directed. It is easy to carry the imagistic approach used in the setting, costumes, and playing of the show, into the publicity. For example, the hearts suggested for *The Boy Friend* can easily be worked into the poster and program cover design. In doing *Once Upon a Mattress*, a wedding cake topped by a crown at a rakish angle could be used on posters and programs, or the program and posters could be designed in the form of a fairy tale book. In *You're a Good Man Charlie Brown* and *Snoopy*, since the director is forbidden under contract to use the "Peanuts" drawings, the poster could show the back gate of a high wooden fence with some childish scrawling on it, or the poster could be in the shape of Snoopy's doghouse with the play's title painted on it and, at the bottom, an open can of paint with paw prints on it. Musicals such as *O, Marry Me* or *All in Love* could have their eighteenth-century settings reflected in types of paper or print for the program with the poster copies from a period "broadside." All of these lend a unique appearance to a production, reflecting the director's individual approach, and are certainly preferable to publicity that emphasizes only the

Broadway production, pointing up the aspects that most amateur performers and budgets could never begin to match.

At the same time, prepackaged publicity material is infinitely preferable
to no publicity. All too often publicity is postponed or forgotten until there
is little time left for imaginative journalism. This is especially true when the
director is responsible for the publicity, as so often is the case in a small-
scale production organization. In addition, a company such as Package
Publicity Service can offer other promotional items, such as buttons, and
table placemats for use in restaurants, which would be difficult for many
groups to create on their own.

FINAL REHEARSALS

A lack of preshow preparation causes the greatest difficulty in the final
rehearsals for a production. Excessive demands on the director and actors
coming from various sources create inflamed tempers, friction, and enormous problems. Some difficulties are bound to arise in a large-scale
production, but if the following suggestions are adhered to, much of the
tension can be avoided.

One difficulty with final rehearsals is that the production staff often asks
too much of the performers at this time. The actors should work with the
completed sets for several rehearsals before they work in costumes and
makeup. The first time they work with the sets and in costumes they should
not be rehearsing the entire show but only an act or a few scenes. They
should have actual properties, not rehearsal properties, to work with for
several rehearsals after they have learned their lines, and should have
adequate time to grow accustomed to the properties before settings and
costumes are added to the rehearsals. The orchestra is usually the last
element to be added, and the first orchestra rehearsal will be tense in
itself—and worse should the director add props, settings, and costumes on
the same evening. The director might want to use the first rehearsal with the
orchestra as a cue-to-cue rehearsal. This type of rehearsal moves from the
end of one musical cue to the start of the next one, omitting dialogue
sections with no musical accompaniment. The advantage of the cue-to-cue
rehearsal is that it places primary emphasis on the musical aspects of the
show, such as smoothing entrances into songs, setting correct tempos, and
establishing proper timing with music played under spoken dialogue. There
is absolutely no reason that the rehearsal schedule cannot be arranged to
introduce each technical element separately, to minimize confusion.

Final rehearsals should also allow time for what is known as a pace
rehearsal. Casts often discover moments of the play that they especially
enjoy and others in which they drag. Song tempos, too, are often
inadvertently slowed by this time. Between the first and second dress
rehearsals a pace rehearsal might be inserted. At this rehearsal all musical

numbers are played faster than usual, and all the actors speak as rapidly as possible, but with clear articulation, overlapping their cues by three words. It soon becomes apparent who knows the lines, cues, and songs, and who does not. Also evident are the performers who cannot make fast adjustments in case anything should go wrong in the actual performance. A pace rehearsal will give the cast a boost of energy; indeed, many performers discover the new clipped tempo is actually the correct one in which their scenes should be played.

A pace rehearsal can also be a boost for cast members who have grown bored with the show by giving them a new situation with which to deal. For this reason, also, guest critics may be brought in for the last two rehearsals. They should be people who understand the nature of dress rehearsals and the production concepts of the director. They should be professional in their outlook, but at the same time kindly toward, and enthusiastic about, what is happening. They should in no way be allowed to weaken cast morale. Even though they are few, the guest critics do constitute an audience, and this allows the cast to play to, and try to please, someone other than the director. No matter how much respect they have for the director, at this point they need a fresh viewpoint.

Always allow time before the final rehearsals and performances for warm-up sessions. This applies to vocal, musical, and physical exercises, so that the cast's energy level will be high and they will be emotionally and physically ready to perform. The following is a sampling of possible warm-up exercises. Exercises should be in this sequence to ensure proper warm-up.

Warm-Up Exercises

Step One: *Stretching the body.* Stand on tiptoes and stretch upward. Bring the arms up and stretch to the fingertips. Pull the chin up, too. Hold a few seconds; then flop over from the waist, bringing the heels back down to the floor. Concentrate on remaining loose, particularly in the neck and shoulder areas. While remaining relaxed in the upper half of the body, gradually "roll up" into a standing position. The head should be the last part to come into place. Repeat three times.

Step Two: *Tension and relaxation.* Lie flat on your back. Imagine that you are a smooth sheet of foil. Concentrate on being as relaxed as possible. Next, imagine that someone picks you up and squeezes you into a tight ball. As you imagine this, draw yourself into a tight mass, occupying a minimum amount of cubic space. Hold a few seconds; then return to the former relaxed state. Give equal time to the state of relaxation. Repeat twice.

Step Three: *Proper breathing.* This step can be done while standing or while lying on your back. Place your hands on the abdominal muscle, the diaphragm. Using a prescribed time count, such as five seconds, inhale, hold the breath, and exhale. Each of the three steps should be given the same time count. Breathe so as to tighten the diaphragm. Do not breathe shallowly or raise your shoulders. Do not tense your throat or shoulder muscles. The only tension should be in the abdominal area. Breathe through open, rounded lips. The first repeat should increase the count, perhaps to eight seconds. The second repeat is extended more, perhaps to ten or twelve seconds.

Step Four: *Breathing and producing sound.* Take a deep breath, being careful not to tense your throat or shoulder muscles. As you exhale, hum a tone on a comfortable pitch. Project the hum against the back row of the audience area. Keep your throat loose and open. Hold the hum as long as the breath allows, but round off the hum evenly at the end to avoid sounding strained. Repeat the steps with the sound "mah." Repeat a second time with the sound "moh."

Step Five: *Articulation.* Say the following phrases with emphasis placed on strong consonant sounds, especially those at the end of words. Repeat each phrase several times, getting increasingly fast but never so fast as to be sloppy. Be sure to remain relaxed and to breathe properly.

"the tip of the tongue on the teeth"
"red leather, yellow leather"
"rubber baby buggy bumpers"
"Mother made Millie, Mollie, and Marie
march many times around the room to
marching music"

Step Six: *Singing.* Combine the relaxation, proper breathing, breath control, projection, and articulation from the previous steps, and sing through portions of one or more songs from the show about to be performed.

If actors do not appear in early scenes of the musical, they can be assigned dressing room time and warm-up exercises after the show has begun. Keep them out of the way of the other actors until that point.

All of the areas we have so far discussed can and should be dealt with before the show begins. Unexpected emergencies are bound to arise in a large-scale production, thus increasing the need for advance preparation. No one needs tension and unpleasant surprises in the home stretch of a production. In fact, if there is any one time when one especially needs a happy and excited outlook in a show, it is the time of the final rehearsals. It is here that, too often, a show is ruined by a lack of proper preparation and the chaos and exhaustion that result. Careful planning, however, can reap the benefits of an excited and enthusiastic cast, a satisfied (if tired) director, and a production capable of delighting audiences.

MUSICALS FOR SPECIAL GROUPS

While everyone knows that children's theatre in the United States is enjoying a great boom, the majority of directors fail to realize that the middle school or junior high school group and the retired persons' group are two of the least tapped and most viable areas for productions, in terms of enthusiastic response to casting calls and attendance. These groups comprise large numbers of interested audience members, and the director should involve them in the productions.

A good musical production for children involves both child and nonchild performers. Far too many directors of children's musicals stage their shows with only adult cast members, in which case the children have very little emotional relationship with any of the characters. The director should also remember that the imagistic approach to staging such musicals works extremely well, since children are generally quick to seize upon symbolism and to accept settings, furnishings, and properties that are not entirely realistic. Their imagination supplies a great deal of decor to simply designed and realized scenic pieces.

In directing child performers, the director must remember that they have short attention spans and should not be required to attend lengthy rehearsals until the final run-throughs. One of the primary rules in producing children's musicals is to rehearse the play in short segments, limiting the time and number of rehearsals involving the child performers. Ideal children's musicals are those that use groups of children, and that also have one or two key roles played by children, in an otherwise adult cast. It is unwise to suppose that just because there is a large turnout of children at auditions for a children's musical, one will be able to cast a great many key parts with talented children. There are simply not many experienced or capable child performers to be found, and the director gets into special difficulties with child cast members, such as transportation, parents who insist on attending all rehearsals but who serve only as distractions for the children, or parents who fail to realize that a child's commitment to a rehearsal schedule must be as strong as an adult's.

It is also advisable to remember that the children need not be kept for the entire rehearsal period. Schedule children for the early section of a rehearsal, use them, and send them on their way. Children who are not receiving direct attention at rehearsals can become distracting to the director and the rest of the cast. A useful technique is to involve two assistant directors, and to assign to one of them the responsibility of caring for all the children at rehearsals and during performances. Otherwise, the children are apt to get in the way of cast and crew. At rehearsals, children should be treated exactly as the adults are treated. The director should hold a meeting with the adult cast members and crew to make certain they understand that they are not to pet or to antagonize the child cast members, so that personality conflicts, based on attention, do not arise. Child cast

Figure 17. Chorus of Children from *Carousel*. As shown in the Valdosta State College production, directed by Randy Wheeler and with scenery design by Joel Boatright, despite the fact that a large-scale musical like *Carousel* depends heavily on the leading performers, it also offers opportunities for large choruses, including groups of children. Photograph by deRon Coppage.

Figure 18. Scene from *Showdown at the Sugarcane Saloon*. In the Valdosta State College production, directed by Randy Wheeler and with scenes designed by Bill Gilbert, the imagistic setting for the children's musical underlines the metaphor of candyland. Bright warm colors in setting and costumes contribute to the effect. Note the exaggerated physical stances and facial expressions, which fit the playing style. Photograph by deRon Coppage.

members will appreciate the respect shown them and will want to earn more of it. In a casting situation, children—even as adults—should be tested to observe their ability for teamwork and imagination.

One effective rehearsal technique, when dealing with children, is a split-focus rehearsal. Such a rehearsal might require child cast members to work with the musical director at 7:00 P.M. When the adult cast members arrive at 7:30, the children leave and work with the director or assistant director in a series of exercises designed to increase the children's awareness of concentration, character development, and control. These sessions are especially beneficial if the children are nonindividualized members of a large chorus.

A continuing development of the character each child plays in the musical can be achieved from week to week in these sessions. For example, at the first session the child may select a name for the character. At the second session the child can describe the character's personality by acting out a scene in which the character enjoys himself or herself, and another in which the character does not. A third session can place the child's character in an improvisational situation with one or more other children. Finally, the character can be placed in the actual scene of the play and allowed to bring out the personality traits developed during the creative sessions. The child actor then feels much more secure in the role, and concentration on stage should be greatly improved.

Listed below is a series of specific exercises that can be used with child actors for warming up and for teaching focus and concentration.

Exercises for Child Performers

Divide the children into two groups. Designate one group *lions* and the other *tigers*. Have the groups form two straight lines, facing each other, on their hands and knees. Give the instruction that each group is to roar and growl, attempting to outroar the opposite group. During the roaring, each child is facing another child directly, but they are never to cross an imaginary center line dividing the two groups.

Divide the children into two groups. Give them a long, heavy rope and have them engage in a tug-of-war. Instruct them to note the placement of their hands and feet during the tug, as well as how they felt as they were engaged in the tugging. Take the rope from them and instruct them to repeat the exercise with an imaginary rope but handling their bodies in the same way as before. A variation on this can involve the tossing of first a real and then an imaginary ball among the children.

Instruct the children to close their eyes and imagine standing in water up to their chins. While keeping their eyes closed, have them move around as if under water, trying to feel the water. Repeat the step with them moving through heavy oil. Repeat a second time, instructing them to move as if in cherry Jell-O.

Divide the children into groups of six to ten. Have each group sit in a circle on the floor. Each group should then select (or be assigned) a category of objects or characters with which to work. Favorites include cartoon characters, movie characters, animals, favorite foods, and vacation spots. One child in each group begins by naming one example in the category. Moving in a clockwise direction, the next child repeats the aforenamed example and adds a second example. The next child repeats the first two examples and adds a third, and so forth. The round continues until someone fails to name the examples in the correct order.

Have the children stand in a large circle. Select one child and send him or her out of sight and hearing range. Select one of the remaining children as the group leader. Have the leader begin a series of simple, repeated body motions that the others in the circle imitate. Instruct the leader to change the motions occasionally without ever coming to a complete halt. The others are to follow the changes out of the corner of their eyes without betraying the identity of the leader. Next, bring back the child sent away and place him or her in the center of the circle. The child's task is to discover the leader by watching and deciding which child is being followed by the others. When the leader is discovered, he or she is sent out, a new leader is selected, and the process begins again.

Divide the children into groups of eight to twelve and have them sit on the floor in a circle, with one person from each group seated in the center of the circle as a control figure. The control figure is then instructed to close his or her eyes. A small object is given to one child in the circle who immediately passes it to the person on the right, who passes it on, and so on, so that the object remains in almost constant motion. At an unspecified time, the child in the center says, "Stop." At this moment, the child holding the object stops passing the object and holds it. The child in the center opens his or her eyes and names a letter of the alphabet to the child holding the object. As soon as the letter is named, the object is again set in quick motion. Before the object is passed once around the group, the child given the letter must name six objects beginning with that letter. If the child fails to do so, then he or she assumes the center seat and the game continues. If the exercise is too difficult for the children, the list of objects can be lowered to three or four. Likewise, if a greater challenge is needed, the list can be lengthened to eight or ten.

Following the warm-up or teaching session with the director and children, the musical director may wish to bring the children back into the choral rehearsal for a brief joint rehearsal so that the adult and child cast members can learn to work together. Chapter 2 of this book contains a list of musicals not only written especially for child audiences, but also that may be adapted for a certain number of child performers, even though the characters may not necessarily be identified as children.

Middle school youngsters present a problem in theatre. They want very much to perform, but there are very few scripts written especially for them. Adolescence is a difficult emotional and physical time; consequently, the strain of lengthy rehearsals can prove too much for middle schoolers. These youngsters are at their best at rehearsals held late in the afternoon, and it is advisable to keep the rehearsals to a period not exceeding one and one-half hours. Chapter 2, the classified list of musicals, suggests shows that can be adapted for this age group. Since this is a transitional group from the standpoint of interests and maturity, the list includes some shows geared more toward the younger side of the group, as well as some that are shows better suited to the more mature youngsters. Certain modifications must be made to some scripts, of course, in dialogue, plot, or actions.

One final thought to keep in mind concerning the use of children and adolescents in a musical is the possibility of adding them to a large chorus that does not necessarily require child cast members. This type of situation works well for both children and director. It allows the child performer to enter a stage-musical experience easily, without undue pressure or demands on talent. For the director, it adds an age depth to the casting that presents a more realistic picture of a musical community, as represented by the chorus. Such shows as *Annie Get Your Gun, Bye Bye Birdie, Carousel, The Music Man*, and *Brigadoon* benefit from child chorus members. Another bonus from this practice comes at the box office, where each child cast member frequently has been the impetus for the sale of a large number of tickets to family and friends.

In staging musicals for the senior adult group we have labeled "retired persons," it is well to remember that the material in the scripts chosen should be familiar to the actors in some way, so that they will feel comfortable in their roles. It is unwise to choose plays in which one performer has a great number of lines to memorize or a great many lines in even one scene. It is helpful to incorporate stage directions, properties, inflections of lines, pronunciations, and even emotional responses of characters at reading rehearsals that precede the blocking of a scene. This will prevent confusion over having too much to absorb at once. Any show with older performers, or intended for an audience of older persons, should definitely have comic elements in it. The ability to elicit laughter from their peers is a great emotional reward for these older performers. Once again, before beginning rehearsals, the director must have a thorough understanding of the play so that direction will stem from a full understanding and interpretation of the material. In working with much older persons, the director may need to adjust the script to the actors and the stage available, and to take every opportunity to minimize strain on the performers. For that reason, the director may want to rely on improvised scripts or revues, especially in the initial work with older performers.

There are, however, a surprising number of scripts with numerous roles for older persons. Readers' theatre presentations of these musicals might be encouraged, provided, of course, that permission to alter the scripts for such performances can be obtained from the production control agencies. The producing organization should write directly to the authors, many of whom will supply the needed permission for such worthwhile projects. The use of a narrator to handle much of the plot, around the occasional playing of a scene or musical number, works especially well in a readers' or chamber theatre approach to the producing of a musical for older persons. These dramatic readings can encourage the use of pantomime, allowing the older person to concentrate on one aspect of the performance. Also, they facilitate the much older person's sustaining energy for the performance.

In directing the older persons' musical, a director must remember that in staging the play an association between a line and its cue is very important, as is the placement of persons near each other in case of hearing or visual difficulties. Movement patterns may also have to be altered for older performers. Exercises in sensory recall may be used effectively during the rehearsal periods. Line-learning sessions may need to be instituted. There is not as much difficulty with the learning process of older persons as many directors might assume, but additional efforts by the director to help make the performers feel comfortable and successful will result in a more satisfying production. In choosing scripts, the director needs, as with any group, to consider the audience's life experiences and backgrounds. Older performers should also be encouraged to participate in all aspects of the production. Set construction, costuming, lighting, properties, and so on will all give the actors a strong sense of full contribution to the production, as well as making them more comfortable in the environment of the production. With slight adaptations, many key roles in musicals can be geared toward older performers, and it is imperative that the director consider characters representative of any ethnic, physical, or disability group.

A list of eight usual problems connected with working with elderly actors follows, along with some suggestions for dealing with those problems.

Retired Persons' Musical Hints

1. Lack of self-confidence can be solved by constant reassurance.
2. Limited reading skill can be supplemented by individual coaching.
3. Senility can be handled by making sure the performer has no lines but is placed strategically in crowd scenes with an accompanying performer guide.
4. Lack of interest can be counteracted by individual contact.
5. Physical disability can be dealt with by limited action, by set design, and by performer guides.

6. Visual impairment can be helped by scripts with large print and individual coaching.
7. Hearing disability can be helped by pairing actors so that one helps the other.
8. Inability to memorize and fear of memorization can be helped by individual coaching and by special line sessions. Also, improvisations give the performers the confidence to ad lib, if necessary.

A list of musicals with roles for older people, and scripts well suited to audiences composed of older people, can be found in the following chapter.

2

THE MUSICALS CLASSIFIED

In categorizing the musicals available for production, no attempt has been made to ascribe the authors or composers or to delineate the plots. The catalogs for the licensing agencies contain that information, and several of the catalogs also detail orchestration. The musicals are listed alphabetically under four headings: Standard Musicals, Children's Musicals, Young Persons' Musicals, and Retired Persons' Musicals. The date of initial New York production follows the title, and the "type" classifications, discussed in Chapter 1 under the heading "Choosing the Musical," are noted. Additionally noted is such information about the musicals as may be helpful to would-be producers and directors in making their selections. We have used the phrase *judicious pruning suggested* when we felt the musical contained expendable material. The last notation refers to the licensing agency. Explanations of codes for types and agencies precede the listings. Agency addresses are given in Chapter 3 of this volume.

Operas and operettas are not included, nor are intimate musical revues, with the exception of those revues with traditional and expositive themes. No standard musical appears unless it is listed as available in agency catalogs. Some once-popular musicals (*Up in Central Park*, for example) are no longer available; some (*A Time for Singing*, *Tovarich*, *Pipe Dream*) are not available because of restrictions on source material; and some have been withdrawn by the agencies in favor of more contemporary versions (as in the case of the withdrawing of *Gentlemen Prefer Blondes* because of its reworking into *Lorelei*).

If a musical is unlisted, it may be possible to secure information on the rights to it from ASCAP, the American Society of Composers, Authors, and Publishers, Lincoln Plaza, New York, New York 10023, (212) 598-3050. Recently, Arena Stage in Washington, D.C., did a sprightly revival of a Marx Brothers oldie, *Animal Crackers*. It took that theatre almost two years to locate fragments of the script—which had been kept by some of the original cast members—and copies of the music before the musical could be reassembled. The result, however, was worth the effort.

Musicals currently running on Broadway (*A Chorus Line*, *Cats*, *Dreamgirls*, *La Cage Aux Folles*, *Little Shop of Horrors*, and *42nd Street*) have also been omitted if rights are not presently available.

Our opinions of the musicals are based on our viewing of them in several productions and production styles, on observations of the reactions of several audiences, and, if the musical has been available for some time, on attendance records in various communities. Where duplications occur in different categories in the following lists, notations are not repeated.

The easiest way to obtain recordings of the musicals is to consult *Simon's Directory* (see the Bibliography), which lists all original cast albums, manufacturing companies, and album order numbers.

Type Classifications

CH: Children's roles

D: Dance show

E: Ensemble show

INT: Intimate production required

LK: Little-known show, not easily recognized by audiences

M: Men's show

SNG: Singers' show

ST: Star show

W: Women's show

Controlling Agencies

A: Anchorage Press

BP: Baker's Plays

CHP: Coach House Press

DPC: Dramatic Publishing Company

MTI: Music Theatre International

PDS: Pioneer Drama Service

PPC: Performance Publishing Company

RH: The Rodgers and Hammerstein Library

SF: Samuel French

TW: Tams-Witmark Music Library

UN: Though listed with a controlling agency, production rights are currently restricted.

STANDARD MUSICALS

The Act (1977) ST
A definitive female star turn, this show is best suited to groups using guest-star performers. It does offer several nonsinging male roles. Strong dance required. Unit set. MTI (UN)

Ain't Supposed to Die a Natural Death (1963) E
Geared to black performers, the show may be too strong in language and attitude for nonurban groups. Ethnic dance. Unit set. SF (UN)

All-American (1962) M
A charming if somewhat overwritten college-set show with good older roles and at least two strong songs: "Once upon a Time" and "Night Life." Athletic dance routines. Many sets. Judicious pruning suggested. TW

Allegro (1947) E, LK
An uneven script has caused this show to be overlooked, which is a pity, because it has an irresistible score ("So Far," "A Fellow Needs a Girl," "The Gentleman Is a Dope"). Strong possibilities for interracial casting. Simple dancing. Suitable for imagistic production. Judicious pruning suggested. RH

All in Love (1963, eighteenth-century source) E, LK
Charming, small-cast musical. Little dance. Simple sets, good imagistic possibilities. MTI

Annie (1977) CH, E
Engaging show, imagistic production possible. Child performers should be double-cast (so should the dog). Strong audience appeal. Little dance. MTI

Annie Get Your Gun (1946) ST, CH, SNG
Fine audience show and a great score, but requires many sets and has only two major women's roles. Lengthy; one complex dance can be eliminated. RH

Anyone Can Whistle (1964) E, LK
Neglected musical with good score, witty, sophisticated script, and a host of character roles. Movement rather than dance. Unit set. MTI

Anything Goes (1934) E, SNG
A top Cole Porter score. The script now available is from the sixties revival, but is still overlong (judicious pruning suggested) and full of unnecessary sets. Tap dancing required. TW

Applause (1970) ST
Bouncy score, distinctly middle-aged roles. Realistic Broadway ambiance is difficult to catch in imagistic production. Extremely sophisticated. TW

The Apple Tree (1966)   INT, E

Three one-act musicals, unfortunately not of equal calibre. Possibilities of different casts for each, otherwise only three central roles and a small chorus. The music is repetitious. Movement rather than dance. Unit set, costumes may be stylized.   MTI

Babes in Arms (1937)   E

One of the greatest of Broadway scores ("Where or When," "Johnny One-Note," "My Funny Valentine," "I Wish I Were in Love Again"), whose tunes have been used in so many different movies that very few remember they're from this one show. A difficult, meandering script, but a strong young-persons' show. Simple dance. A set must be dismantled in the audience's view during each performance.   RH

Bajour (1964)   D, E, LK

Interesting plot (gypsies in Manhattan), but unpleasant characters. Not much appeal. Judicious pruning suggested.   DPC

Baker Street (1965)   ST, D

Charming show for middle-aged (and older) performers. Lends itself to imagistic production, but needs excellent dancers.   SF

Barnum (1979)   ST

Wonderful imagistic possibilities, nice score, but the show must have a male lead who is an athlete as well as a singer. Without him, the show is considerably weakened.   TW

Bells Are Ringing (1956)   ST

Virtually a one-role (female lead) show; has dated rather badly. Might serve as a period piece (costumed and set in the 1950s). Tuneful, but also dated, score. Judicious pruning suggested.   TW

Ben Franklin in Paris (1964)   M, ST, LK

Appealing, but distinctly middle-aged central roles, and a tuneful, pro-American score. Elaborate stage effects (a balloon ride over Paris) and costume requirements. Little dance.   SF

Berlin to Broadway with Kurt Weill (1972)   E, INT

One of the best cabaret shows. Lovely music with both a European and American flavor. Possibilities of audience interplay. Simple dance.   MTI

Best Foot Forward (1941)   E

Lovely period piece for youngsters: can be set in the late 1930s, 1940s, or 1950s. The early-1960s revival added some songs and combined several roles for Liza Minnelli. Take a look at the original script; it's better. Judicious pruning suggested.   TW

The Best Little Whorehouse in Texas (1978)   E
May be too raunchy and bawdy for the nonurban public, but, once again, the rousing stage version far surpasses the movie. Excellent imagistic production; distinctly middle-aged leads. TW (UN)

Bloomer Girl (1944)   W
Lilting score, but elaborate sets and costumes are necessary for this sentimental Civil War fable. Expense has caused it to be overlooked, but if you can afford it, it's worth doing. The ballet can be cut.   TW

The Boy Friend (1954 spoof of 1920s musicals)   E, D
You can't go wrong with this stylish, funny, melodic satire. Strong choreography helps.   MTI

The Boys from Syracuse (1938)   M, SNG
This perky version of Shakespeare's *A Comedy of Errors* was revived in an imagistic production off-Broadway in the early 1960s. Pleasing score, but the first act ends with a long, dreary ballet. The period costumes are relatively simple. A potential problem lies in finding four male look-alikes who can pass for two sets of twins. Judicious pruning suggested.   RH

Brigadoon (1947)   SNG
Cannot be done without elaborate sets and lighting and period Scottish costumes, but how often do you find scores that include such gems as "There But for You Go I" and "I'll Go Home with Bonnie Jean," in addition to the better-known "Almost Like Being in Love" and "The Heather on the Hill"? Some of the dances (created originally to cover scene changes) can be cut, and this overlong musical needs cutting to sustain the fantasy.   TW

Bring Back Birdie (1980)   E, D
Unsuccessful sequel to *Bye Bye Birdie*.   TW

Bye Bye Birdie (1960)   E, D
A sprightly look at the 1950s phenomenon of rock and roll and a sure audience pleaser. Multitudinous sets and realistic props. Period choreography.   TW

By Jupiter (1942)   E, LK
This appealing show has somehow been overlooked, although it had a presentable Broadway run. Good for college and community theatre, and its women's lib plot is very topical. Easy to do in imagistic production.   RH

By the Beautiful Sea (1951)   ST
Nice bit of American nostalgia, but definitely a vehicle for a woman star, and there's no way around a lavish production—a balloon ascent and a turn-of-the-century midway. Good 1900s costuming a necessity. Pretty score; good black roles.   MTI

Cabaret (1966)   E

Don't be misled by the movie: This is *not* a star show for an ingenue; indeed, it offers strong roles for older performers. The production is very easy to do imagistically and the orchestra's inclusion in the action is optional. May be a little strong for some communities. Has 1930s dance.   TW

Calamity Jane (variety of dates)   ST, LK

A 1953 Doris Day movie, turned into a stage vehicle for newcomer Carol Burnett in the early 1960s (but for stock only), then into a TV special for her. It's pokey onstage, but has some good music ("Secret Love," "The Deadwood Stage") and is good for high school. Little dance.   TW

Call Me Madam (1950)   ST

Very dated now, but could be done as a nostalgia piece (the late 1940s). Impossible to do without a great many sets and costumes. Only two women's roles of any size. Not much dance.   MTI

Camelot (1960)   M

Great audience appeal, but overwritten and uneven to a surprising degree. Can use an imagistic setting, but requires strong costumes, and has only one major female role. There's no denying it has a gorgeous and lush score. Little dance.   TW

Can-Can (1953)   D

If you've got dancers, try it, after you prune it. Nice, brassy Cole Porter score, but boring script. Has to have sets and costumes elaborate enough to suggest Paris in 1900, or it won't work. Strong dance required.   TW

Candide (1956, 1973)   SNG, E

Rousing, but difficult, score; much appreciated by young audiences. Easy to stylize sets and costumes (stick to the later script and score), but top voices are a must.   MTI

Canterbury Tales (1969)   E

Cute idea; might appeal to college groups, and easy to stylize. The rock music has dated badly and the tales selected for the American production are too similar and become monotonous. Stylized movement rather than dance.   MTI

Carnival (1961)   M, SNG

Why is this musical being neglected? Pretty score and energetic production possibilities. Easy to stylize and great audience appeal. Only two women's roles of any importance, and the ingenue needs a glorious voice. Dancing, mostly male.   TW

Carousel (1945)   SNG

One of the great ones, but very long. Elaborate sets demanded (the ambiance of the carnival midway is a must); also strong voices and a large cast. Costuming is also expensive and necessary to 1900s atmosphere. Don't be afraid to take scissors to some of the long dance interludes.   RH

Celebration (1968)   INT
Certainly one of the strongest opening numbers in musicals, and a stylized production. Suitable to high school and community groups. It becomes repetitious, and the music is never up to the opening. Little dance.   MTI

Chicago (1975)   INT, D
Why does this musical, made from the warm and funny film *Roxie Hart*, seem so cold and heartless? A stylistic production, full of unpleasant characters. Best suited to an urban audience. Heavy dancing.   SF

Cindy (1962)   INT
This little gem of a young persons' musical had a vogue in the early 1960s, appeared in the late 1970s as a TV special for black performers, and seems to have vanished. Nice, stylized production, cute score, little dance, worth doing.   TW

Company (1970)   E
Strong score, stylized production; requires actors who can act, sing, and dance. Not easy to cast, but thought-provoking for mature audiences. Virtually unplayable on high school or junior college level.   MTI

Curley McDimple (1967)   E, CH
An amusing spoof of old Shirley Temple films for audiences who can recognize the type. Cast can be expanded; the production is stylized. Fun for film-buff communities, but over the heads of younger players. Little dance.   SF

Dames at Sea (1968)   D, INT
Another movie spoof: this time of Busby Berkley's 1930s Gold Digger movies. This, however, works well on its own. Catchy score, cast can be expanded. Unit sets, 1930s costuming. No need to double roles, as the original production did.   SF

Damn Yankees (1955)   M
Overlong for today's audiences and rather dated in tone and music. A great deal of the dancing isn't really necessary. The basic plot premise is too sophisticated for high schoolers. Good older roles.   MTI

Dearest Enemy (1925)   E, LK
Another overlooked gem (the score includes "Here in My Arms"). Historical setting (the American Revolution) with good character roles. Period sets and costumes a necessity, but worth reviving. Not a dance show.   RH

Dear World (1969)   W

There's no pretending that *The Madwoman of Chaillot* works as a musical: The score isn't much and the philosophy is earthbound. A group that includes plenty of character women might consider it, but might be better to do the nonmusical version. Little dance.   TW

Diamond Studs (1976)   M, LK

Jesse James rides again, to music. A good deal of fun and full of country/western appeal; strong publicity possibilities. Stylized production possible, costumes can also be stylized. Western dance.   SF

Do I Hear a Waltz? (1965)   W, E, LK

The musical version of *The Time of the Cuckoo* doesn't quite make it, but it's too bad, for it's a nice show for older performers and has a lilting score. Try it, and edit it: It'll please mature audiences. Imagistic sets can capture Venice more easily than realistic ones did.   RH

Donnybrook (1961)   M, LK

Stage version of the film *The Quiet Man*; suitable if you have to do a musical around St. Patrick's Day, but otherwise forgo it. The material cries out for the real glories of Ireland's countryside. The score is not memorable. Ethnic dance and a lengthy choreographed fistfight.   SF

Don't Bother Me, I Can't Cope! (1972)   E, INT

Extremely urban in tone and appeal; won't work away from urban audiences. Easy to stylize; cast can be expanded. Ethnic movement.   SF

Drat! The Cat (1965)   E, LK

A nice takeoff on turn-of-the-century melodramas, with an up-and-down score ("He Touched Me"). Good for high schools and community college groups. Stylized sets and costumes. Little dance.   SF

Dubarry Was a Lady (1939)   ST

Demands a strong female lead and a strong comic male lead. Much of the music has gone into revivals of other shows (for example, "Friendship" into *Anything Goes* revival). Elaborate sets and costumes. Little dance.   TW

The Education of H*Y*M*A*N K*A*P*L*A*N (1968)   E

Good for older groups; possibilities for simple production. Urban in tone, stylized movement rather than dance.   DPC

Ernest in Love (1960)   E

A musical version of *The Importance of Being Earnest* and pleasant for a group capable of catching its style. Has 1900s sets (but few) and costumes (but simple). Good bet.   MTI

Fade Out—Fade In (1964)   ST, M
Carol Burnett didn't like this, her last Broadway vehicle, and so, alas, she has never returned to the Great White Way. It's not much of a show, and one piece of music turns up again in *Hallelujah, Baby.* Dance is simple.   TW

A Family Affair (1962)   E
Very ethnic and urban; not many possibilities in this loose and overlong tale of a coming wedding. Little dance.   MTI

Fanny (1954)   SNG, M
This overblown and overlong piece worked better as a movie (without the score—and that's too bad, because it's lovely). Sets, and cast demands, make it difficult. Good older roles.   TW

The Fantasticks (1960)   M, INT
Without saying—it can't fail. You can be as inventive as you like with the simplistic costumes, setting, and staging. Movement rather than dance.   MTI

Fashion (1845, 1970)   E, W
Excellent for women's groups and schools. Only one man (a director), who tries to stage the early American play with an all-female cast. Great fun. Simple sets, movement.   SF

Fiddler on the Roof (1964)   ST, E
Don't think of it as ethnic; it's all-humanity, and a sure hit. Many sets and costumes; large cast required.   MTI

Finian's Rainbow (1947)   M
A lilting score and clever idea, but times have changed and the theme has become tasteless. Too bad.   TW

Fiorello! (1959)   ST
Very hard to do, for non-New York audiences don't remember the title character. A large character cast; many necessary sets and costumes. Overlong. Ethnic dance sequence.   TW

First Impressions (1959)   W
Easy-to-stylize version of *Pride and Prejudice,* but good costumes a must. An uneven score, but good young persons' show. Simple dance.   SF

Flower Drum Song (1958)   E
Not one of Rodgers and Hammerstein's better works. Confused plot, too many characters, numerous elaborate sets and costumes. Might work for high school groups, but the idea of making up Caucasians for roles better played by Orientals is not appealing today.   RH

Follies (1971)   E
A wonderful show for older groups. Stylization of set possible, costumes contemporary, except for ghostly characters. Marvel-

ous score. A very bitter tone from the original production can be offset by direction and playing. Good choreography necessary.   MTI

Frank Merriwell (1971)   E, M, LK
One of those Broadway failures that younger groups can have great fun with. Turn-of-the-century costumes, but sets can be imagistic. Nice score; little dance.   SF

Funny Girl (1964)   ST, M
Almost impossible to shake the Streisand memory. A large cast and elaborate sets, dance, and costumes, but a one-performer show.   TW

A Funny Thing Happened on the Way to the Forum (1962)   M
A simple set, stylized costumes, and a fine score; a funny crowd-pleaser. It's somewhat chauvinistic, but this can be downplayed.   MTI

George M (1969)   ST, D
Nice, stylized piece, but must have the male lead to carry the vehicle. 1900-1940 costumes, but easy to imagize the physical production. Tap and specialty dance required.   TW

Gigi (1973)   E
A great deal of audience appeal, but the stage version is not up to the movie. Easy to create an imagistic set, but elaborate costumes (Paris, 1900) are a must. Wonderful score; vocal arrangements are more difficult than for the film. Little dance.   TW

Girl Crazy (1930)   E
This musical has had a big comeback and the score is worth it ("Embraceable You," "Fascinating Rhythm," "Bidin' My Time"), but most revivals simply point out how long and trite the script has become. Edit and stylize the production. Good show for youngsters. Little dance.   TW

Godspell (1971)   E
Still works, but rethink it: It does not have to be about hippie clowns. Great audience appeal, particularly for church and young groups. Set and costumes can be any style. Some dance.   MTI

The Golden Apple (1954)   SNG
Complicated show. For experienced musical groups only. In general the music ("Lazy Afternoon") makes up for an unwieldy and overlong book. Complicated sets and turn-of-the-century costumes. Minimal dance required.   TW

Golden Boy (1968)   ST
Possible for groups with good black performers, but the score is less than distinguished, and the book very dated. Many sets: can't be stylized. Fight scene, which needs to be choreographed as an encapsulated boxing match. Some dance.   SF

Golden Rainbow (1963)   ST
Musical version of *A Hole in the Head*, written for Steve Lawrence and Eydie Gorme. Difficult to handle.   SF

Goldilocks (1953)   E
This tale of early movies has some fine tunes ("I Never Know When to Say When"), but simply meanders through too many sets, costumes, and characters. Little dance. Little audience appeal.   SF

Good News (1927, 1974)   M
Terrific score ("The Best Things in Life Are Free," "Lucky in Love"), but the revised and better version (TW) is not available to amateur groups, and the version that is (SF) is very dated and cumbersome. Has 1930s sets, costumes, and dance.   TW/SF

Goodtime Charley (1975)   ST, LK
A musical about Joan of Arc. Really unplayable.   SF

The Grand Tour (1974)   ST, LK
Little-known and lovely score, but the plot and characters go everywhere (sets) and nowhere (dramatically). Long dance numbers requiring a large chorus.   SF

The Grass Harp (1971)   W, INT
A truly glorious score, a cast of character performers. It's surprising that this one isn't better known. Stylized sets, noncontemporary look in costumes. Movement rather than dance.   SF

Grease (1972)   E
A great show for the younger groups, if you can clean up the language and the male chauvinistic ending. Tremendous audience appeal. Stylized set, 1950s costuming and dances.   SF

Guys and Dolls (1950)   M
One of the American classics; easy to do in an imagistic set. Not quite contemporary in tone; do it as a period (1950s) piece. One complicated, strong dance, and simple nightclub routines.   MTI

Gypsy (1959) ST, W, CH

Many sets, quick set changes, combination of the realistic and the stylized, period (1930s) costumes, lots of child performers, and overlong. A central woman's role requiring a star turn. For sophisticated and monied producers only. TW

Hair (1968) E

The trend-setting rock musical has aged badly. Might make it as a period piece, but this type of nostalgia would probably produce yawns. The nudity was never really necessary, simply exhibitionistic. TW

Half a Sixpence (1965) E, D

This little gem of a musical is discussed fully earlier in the text. It is not, as many think, a star vehicle, and offers a good variety of character roles. Good for Christmas holiday performances. Keep the peppy dances; they help. DPC

Hallelujah, Baby (1967) ST

The sojourn of a black actress through time never quite worked. Peppy score and some good numbers don't make up for the dreary book. Easy to stylize, if you have the leading lady. Pre-Civil War to mid-1960s. Dances must evoke specific eras. MTI

Happy Hunting (1956) ST

Not much hope for this faded musical about a socialite who doesn't get an invitation to the Kelly-Rainier wedding. A period piece but the score isn't much, except for "Mutual Admiration Society." MTI

The Happy Time (1968) M, D, CH

Easy to stylize, lots of youngsters' roles, and a melodic score. The subject of the play, which is a warm family musical about a photographer, suggests the use of projections. Strong dancing. TW

Hello, Dolly! (1964) ST, D

One of the major American musicals, with a large cast and turn-of-the-century costumes. A great crowd pleaser and easy to stylize, but you have to have the leading lady and choreographer. TW

Henry, Sweet Henry (1967) W

Based on the fine film *The World of Henry Orient*, but lacking nearly everything that the film had. Book and score are weak, but there are a variety of roles for midteens. Can be staged with the use of projections. SF

Here's Love (1963) CH

One of the many versions of *Miracle on 34th Street*, this one comes closer to the movie's success than most. A holiday possibility, but difficult to stage—the numbers include a Macy's parade. Many sets, and does not lend itself to imagistic production. MTI

High Button Shoes (1947)   E, D
This is another of the overlooked musicals. Nice score includes "I Still Get Jealous" and "Papa, Won't You Dance with Me?" There is a long Keystone Cops dance number which can't be cut as it makes plot points. It's a lovely family show, and some good central roles for older players. Easy to imagize. TW

High Spirits (1964)   W
The musical version of *Blithe Spirit*, a peppy script. Lots of lush sets and difficult special effects (including flying ghosts), nice score, and wonderful older roles. Not much dancing. TW

Hit the Deck (1927)   M
It might be time to serve this up again as a period piece. Easy to stylize and a top score ("Hallelujah," "Sometimes I'm Happy"). Needs the dance numbers. TW

How Now, Dow Jones (1967)   E
There really is not much to recommend this tasteless trifle, except a catchy song, "Step to the Rear." The appeal is strictly New York. One big production number. SF

How to Succeed in Business without Really Trying (1961)   M
Easy to stylize, nice score, but the production has become dated. Not firm enough for a period piece. Stylized movement rather than dance. MTI

I Can Get It for You Wholesale (1962)   E
Stage version of a novel, with all of the faults of the original. Introduced Barbra Streisand in a supporting role, but that's its only claim to fame. Very episodic and too local (New York's garment district) to have much appeal elsewhere. Little dance. TW

I Do, I Do (1966)   INT, ST
Wonderful score and charming story of a marriage; easy to stylize; great audience pleaser. So, what's wrong with it? Only two players in the cast. Little dance required. MTI

Illya Darling (1967)   ST
Stage version of the movie *Never on Sunday*, which displayed the vibrant scenery of Greece. That's not possible for the stage. Very limited appeal. Ethnic dance numbers. TW

I Love My Wife (1977)   INT, E
Imagistic production, sparkling score ("Hello, Good Times"), small cast. It's doubtful that the central theme of group sex will work in most locales, however. Stylized movement rather than dance. The musicians are among the performers.   SF

I Married an Angel (1938)   E
Cumbersome fantasy; difficult to stage today. Technical problems (flying heroine) and dated dialogue.   RH

Irene (1919, 1974)   ST
Don't delude yourself; the revival script is no better than the original. Fine score with additions for the revival ("Alice Blue Gown," "I'm Always Chasing Rainbows"), but only two major women's roles: one ingenue, one character. Lots of sets, period costumes. Long dance numbers.   TW

Irma La Douce (1960)   INT, M, D
Bright little show, best remembered as a nonmusical movie. Only one major female role, probably the reason more groups don't do it. Strong dance.   TW

It's a Bird . . . It's a Plane . . . It's Superman (1966)   M, LK
No connection with the movie, but probably the movie's success would have revived the musical were it not for the enormous technical difficulties inherent in the script. (*He* has to fly). Meandering book and too many extraneous characters.   TW

Jacques Brel Is Alive and Well and Living in Paris (1968)   E, INT
Audiences love this melodic revue; cast can be somewhat expanded, but good and versatile singers are required.   MTI

Jesus Christ, Superstar (1971)   M, SNG
Disassociate yourself from the glitz of the Broadway production and the fact that some think it "shocking." It can be done simply in a variety of imaginative ways and it isn't at all irreverent. Allows for expanded or small cast, and audiences find it very appealing.   MTI

Joseph and the Amazing Technicolor Dreamcoat (1970/1982)   M, SNG
Material added (music and dialogue) for the Broadway version—twelve years after the original choral version—improves it enormously. Wonderful audience response and you can be as imaginative in stylizing the production as you want. No possibility of expanding the few women's roles.   MTI

The King and I (1951)   ST, CH, D
Really easy to stylize, and a "can't miss," with a score full of hits. Costumes will be expensive, and oriental makeup is required. A large cast, but the children's roles are endearing crowd pleasers. Dance is critical to mood.   RH

Kismet (1953)   ST, SNG

Easy to produce imagistically, but the music is difficult. Don't try it unless you have top singers loaded with personality. Long, and rather humorless. Elaborate costuming required. Some dance.   MTI

Kiss Me, Kate (1948)   M, SNG

Story of Broadway actors playing in a musical version of *Taming of the Shrew*. Intricate sets and costumes for both backstage and onstage action. A top Cole Porter score; sophisticated. Dances are important.   TW

Knickerbocker Holiday (1958)   M, SNG

A neglected musical worthy of a revival, particularly if a group wants a historic musical about the Dutch settlement of New York. Costumes will be an expense, but the production can be stylized easily. Some dance.   RH

Lady Audley's Secret (1971)   E, LK

This musical has been very successful in out-of-New York repertory companies. A bit long, but lilting musically and the melodrama spoóf is easy to stylize. Late nineteenth-century period costumes. Little dancing.   MTI

Lady in the Dark (1941)   ST, SNG

The dream sequences can be stylized, but there are still many "realistic" sets, a large cast, and difficult music. Unfortunately, the denouement—that a woman, to be a success, must give up career for a family—is likely to be soundly booed today. Stylized movement rather than dance.   TW

The Last Sweet Days of Isaac (1970)   INT, LK

Rather limited in appeal; stylized production. Low key emotionally for both characters and audience.   SF

Leave It to Jane (1917, 1960)   E, INT

Great fun for younger casts. Simple sets, and a nostalgic turn, with none of the "camp" of some revivals. The lovely Kern score is a big plus. Sprightly period dancing.   TW

Li'l Abner (1956)   E

The score is better than one remembers, and the comic strip suggests easy stylization for the production, but the script is unfocused—too many conflicting plots, and so many major characters that the central characters get lost. Long Sadie Hawkins ballet. Major requirement: a very tall, muscular leading male who sings well.   TW

Little Mary Sunshine (1959)   INT, E, SNG

This spoof of operettas borders on "camp," but audiences always enjoy it. Very simple dances, sets, and costumes, several good older roles.   SF

Little Me (1962)   ST

A really sharp score ("A Real Live Girl," "I've Got Your Number," "The Other Side of the Tracks"), but an elaborate physical production is required and costumes cover a fifty-year period. Best done with the same male in all key roles. It is possible to stylize it, but the production values enhance a lackluster script. Dancing opportunities are mostly solos; the major ensemble dance can be cut.   TW

A Little Night Music (1972)   E, SNG

Gorgeous score and easy to stylize. A recognizable hit ("Send in the Clowns") can help publicize the show, but there is a cold tone to the script that sometimes causes audiences to admire rather than love.   MTI

Lock Up Your Daughters (1969)   M, LK

This British musical has never gotten much of a play in the States, but it is a bawdy romp and the score is tangy. Dances are athletic rather than demanding, but the vehicle is only for sophisticated audiences.   SF

Lorelei (1974)   ST

The flashback device of the script makes this production simple to stylize. It has the best of *Gentlemen Prefer Blondes* (especially the score), without the cumbersome plot and sets. Period costume (1920s) and a definite star vehicle. Not much dance required.   TW

Lost in the Stars (1949)   E, SNG

A moving plot, sublime score, and a cast that allows for a powerful combination of white and black actors. Stylization possible. Long neglected. Dance minimal.   RH

Lovely Ladies, Kind Gentlemen (1970)   M

This musical version of *The Teahouse of the August Moon* has little to recommend it—what it does have is the script, but producers can more easily do the nonmusical source. No dance to speak of; no women's roles; weak score.   SF

Mack and Mabel (1974)   ST, M, D

Easily stylized (use of film clips possible), excellent score ("When Mabel Walks In the Room," "I Won't Send Roses," "Tap Your Troubles Away"). The book is trouble and the costumes (1915-1925) must be both realistic and evocative of the films of the period, but it's worth doing. Tap required.   SF

The Mad Show (1966)   E, INT

This delightful revue dated too quickly, as satires will. An off-Broadway hit in the mid-1960s, internal problems kept it from being released until the mid-1970s, by which time its vogue was over. It's very expensive in royalty, and audiences just don't catch the humor nowadays.   SF

Maggie Flynn (1968)   ST, M, CH, SNG, LK

A sprawling Civil War musical with lots of roles for black children. Lovely and unknown score; little dance. Period costumes and many sets; not easily stylized.   SF

Mame (1966)   W, CH, ST

This show has been fully discussed in Chapter 1. Audiences love it, but the production is expensive. The major child should be double-cast; the dance is difficult and necessary; and the leading lady must sing, act, and dance.   TW

Man of La Mancha (1965)   M, SNG

The set difficulty for this stylized show has been previously discussed. The play is fine, and audiences respond strongly. The female lead (difficult singing and dancing) is more of a casting problem than the male lead. No other major women's roles to speak of, and the dancing is difficult.   TW

The Man with a Load of Mischief (1966)   INT, E, SNG

Ignored gem. Fine score and charming characters in an engrossing plot. Little dance, period costumes, simple sets. Try it.   SF

Me and Juliet (1953)   E, LK

Not one of Rodgers and Hammerstein's better efforts, though the score has such hits as "No Other Love," "Keep It Gay," and "Marriage Type Love." It does offer an interesting glimpse of backstage activity for a nonknowledgeable audience. Some of the songs ("Intermission Talk") date it badly. The dance is extraneous.   RH

The Me Nobody Knows (1970)   INT, E, SNG

Urban, contemporary dance required. Young people will enjoy working on this show. Easily imagized.   SF

Merrily We Roll Along (1982)   E, SNG

The critics slaughtered it, but it's a fine young-persons' show with a strong lesson about life, and the Sondheim score is superb. Movement rather than dance; stylized production.   MTI

Milk and Honey (1961)   LK, SNG, E

Fine but challenging score; almost all central roles are older characters. The plot is antique. Could be done as a nostalgia piece about the early days of the state of Israel. Can't be stylized. Ethnic dancing a must.   TW

Minnie's Boys (1970)   M, ST, LK

The story of the Marx brothers' youth has some top songs ("Mama a Rainbow," "Be Happy") but an impossible script, and the casting of the Marx brothers is difficult. Has 1915 to 1930 sets, costumes, and dances.   SF

Mr. President (1962)   M
Long, long, long salute to American politics. A neglected
Berlin score, though some of the numbers have dated badly.
Might be done as a salute to the early 1960s, but the many sets
make it really too expensive to consider. Dancing is very dated.
MTI

Mr. Wonderful (1956)   ST
Virtually a nightclub act for the central performer (originally
black, Sammy Davis, Jr., but the role need not be ethnic).
Nightclub atmosphere is easy to set and stage; dancing is
simple.   MTI

The Most Happy Fella (1956)   M, SNG
Almost an opera. Long, and the music is very difficult, the
dance minimal. Some strong roles for mature actors. Too
difficult for many groups.   MTI

The Music Man (1957)   ST, CH
The "Seventy-Six Trombones" musical can't miss with audiences. It offers a lot of roles for midteens, and the dancing is
strong, but the costumes and sets auger an expensive production. The length can be a problem unless the director can really
move it along. A good show for using all ages in the
cast.   MTI

My Fair Lady (1955)   ST, SNG, M
A fine, but expensive, audience show. Not much dance; a
female lead who must really sing. Difficult to do in imagized
production, and the costuming must be turn-of-the-century
and sumptuous. For groups that really have a big budget.
TW

New Girl in Town (1957)   ST, D
The musical version of *Anna Christie* is up-and-down. (The
"up" is the dancing, the "down" is everything else.)
"Sunshine Girl" is a peppy song, but the score is otherwise
lackluster. Turn-of-the-century costumes, and the production
won't really permit stylization, which makes it expensive.
MTI

No, No, Nanette (1925, 1971)   D, W
A wonderful women's show and great audience favorite. Only
three sets, and the costumes are not difficult. The cast must
capture the style of the revival script set in the 1920s (not easy),
but one of the definite money-makers for a group. Period
dance is a must.   TW

No Strings (1961)   M, ST, LK

Interesting plot, and stylization possibilities galore, but the female lead must be black and other roles cannot be, which creates casting difficulties. Although not a costume show, the clothes for the central female, a top fashion model, demand a good deal of panache, and the bittersweet tone limits audience appeal.   RH

Of Thee I Sing (1932)   M

Revivals of this landmark musical viewed recently have demonstrated clearly that its day is done. Its points of satire no longer exist, so the audience has no frame of reference. Many sets and characters; a nice score; 1930s dancing required.   SF

Oh, Captain (1958)   ST, M

Many remember the happy film *The Captain's Paradise*. Unfortunately, neither the nonmusical nor the musical stage version works. Episodic and repetitious. Score doesn't help; some extraneous dancing.   TW

Oh, Coward (1972)   E, SNG, INT, LK

Easy to stylize a production of this revue based on the works of the multitalented Noel Coward. Original cast of three can be expanded slightly. Some dance, but for sophisticated audiences only.   MTI

Oh, Kay (1926)   M, LK

Peppy musical featuring "Someone to Watch over Me" and "Clap Your Hands," could easily be as popular as *No, No, Nanette* in a stylized revival. The plot smacks of *The Boy Friend*, but that's not a fault, and there are opportunities for expansion of period dances.   TW

Oklahoma! (1943)   E, D, SNG

A real winner! Very few sets and, in this day of country/western clothing popularity, easy to costume. Take a look at the dream ballet. Is it too long? Does it really need to be danced by performers different from the leads? The ballet was a groundbreaker in its day, but can be a bore to today's viewers if not handled well.   RH

Oliver (1963)   Ch, M

A unit set and simple costumes. Lots of child roles and sprightly dances, plus a fine score. Only one large female role. Little girls can be cast in some boys' roles.   TW

On a Clear Day You Can See Forever (1968)   ST, M, LK

Nice score, but many sets, some early nineteenth-century costumes, and a jerky script. Intriguing premise but the plot wanders, and that's too bad, for there's something here. Little dance.   TW

Once upon a Mattress (1959)   ST, M, LK

>   A surefire audience pleaser. Easy to do in a unit set; dances are
>   not complicated, costumes are simpler than you first suppose,
>   and the score is much better than you may remember. You
>   have to have the female lead, but it doesn't have to be a Carol
>   Burnett type.   RH

110 in the Shade (1963)   M

>   The musical version of *The Rainmaker* just doesn't jell. The
>   dances seem forced, and the score is weak. The basic material is
>   antimusical. Too many sets; only one woman's role of any
>   importance.   TW

One Touch of Venus (1943)   ST

>   This musical fantasy hasn't aged well. Nice score ("That's
>   Him" and the haunting "Speak Low"). Elaborate dances
>   include two long ballets. Many sets, high-fashion costuming.
>   TW

On the Town (1944)   E, D

>   Done as a salute to the 1940s, this happy musical might prove a
>   good bet. Sets can be stylized, and costumes are on the simple
>   side, but you'd better have good dancers.   TW

On the Twentieth Century (1978)   SNG, M, ST

>   If you have a lot of money to spend, the audience can go out
>   singing the praises of the lovely sets. That's about all there is to
>   recommend this pokey, tuneless, and overlong show.   SF

On Your Toes (1936, 1954, 1983)   E, D

>   This musical keeps being revived on Broadway, but the book
>   never gets better. Nice, tinkly score ("There's a Small Hotel,"
>   "Quiet Night"), and a long, difficult ballet ("Slaughter on
>   Tenth Avenue"). Can't be unit set and the costumes need to be
>   1930s. Judicious pruning suggested.   TW

Out of This World (1950)   E, LK

>   A fine and forgotten Cole Porter score, but the production
>   needs elaborate sets, costumes, and stage effects (for example,
>   Juno's chariot, Mercury's flying). Worth trying if you have
>   sophisticated patrons. Judicious pruning suggested.   TW

Over Here (1974)   ST, INT, LK

>   If you can think of this as 1940s nostalgia and not a star vehicle
>   for the Andrews sisters, you can make a hit with it. The score is
>   fine (though it needs a "big band" sound), the setting is
>   simple, as are the costumes, and audiences love the hijinks. The
>   period dances are not difficult and, after all the fun that's gone
>   before, the ending still causes a mist of audience tears.
>   Worthwhile.   SF

Pacific Overtures (1976)   M, SNG

This musical history of the industrialization of Japan is a very unlikely audience draw for any group.   MTI

Paint Your Wagon (1952)   M, SNG

Such a beautiful score ("I Talk to the Trees," "I Still See Elisa," "Another Autumn," "They Call the Wind Maria"), but the book wanders noticeably. Only one woman's role of any importance. The dancing is western and athletic. Forget the movie; there's little similarity.   TW

Pajama Game (1954)   E, D

Still a top score, but this story of a possible factory strike has dated. Might be done as a 1950s tribute. Dancing isn't easy, and there are many complicated sets.   MTI

Pal Joey (1940)   ST, W, D

The movie softened the script considerably. Most audiences are not enthralled by an evening full of venal and boorish characters who exhibit no redeeming virtues. Many sets could be stylized; the dancing is simple.   RH

Peter Pan (1954)   St, CH

More of a play with music than a musical. Don't do it unless you have the technical equipment for the flying and the many involved sets. Costume expense also required; staging rather than choreographing of the musical numbers.   SF

Pippin (1972)   E, D

This musical seems to have found a home with high school and college groups, who don't object to its slight script and who concentrate instead on the appealing score. Unit set; feudal period costumes; complex dancing.   MTI

Plain and Fancy (1955)   E, LK

This pleasant Amish musical has a nice score and is good for family audiences, but there are many sets, and some problem stage devices (driving a car onstage) that can't be cut. Dancing is minimal.   SF

Pretzels (1972)   E, INT, LK

An unpretentious musical revue. Humor hasn't held up.   SF

Promenade (1969)   INT, E, LK

Pops up occasionally with groups just beginning to produce musicals, but not much appeal.   SF

Promises, Promises (1969)   M

Lots of sets; some difficult dancing in this stage musical based on the film *The Apartment*. The Burt Bacharach score has dated quickly.   SF

Purlie (1970)   M

Not as funny as it once was, and the hippie white youth's character is dated now. Cast mostly black. Fine score, some dance; many sets.   SF

Raisin (1973)   E, SNG

Unit set musical. Mostly black characters. Score is not memorable; dance is an intrusion. The source material, *A Raisin in the Sun*, doesn't suit a musical.   SF

Redhead (1959)   ST, LK, D

Turn-of-the-century costumes and many sets required. The leading lady should be a fine dancer (a Gwen Verdon show not many people remember). Score is pleasant but undistinguished.   MTI

Rex (1976)   ST, M, CH

Not one of Richard Rodgers' best, and quite possibly his weakest. Can be unit set, but requires elaborate Elizabethan costumes. Little dance; might have some appeal for schools.   RH

Riverwind (1963)   E, INT, LK

A neglected musical for a small cast, mostly character performers. Unit set; no dance to speak of. Worth doing.   MTI

The Roar of the Greasepaint, the Smell of the Crowd (1965)   ST, INT

A top score ("On a Wonderful Day Like Today," "The Joker Is Me") isn't helped by an impoverished book dealing with British cultural problems unrelated to American audiences. Lots of youngsters' roles; simple set and costumes; not much dance.   TW

The Robber Bridegroom (1976)   E, SNG, LK

Should be done more often than it is, as it's a great folk music show, allowing for inventive staging. A small cast, unit set, simple costumes, and the audience responds strongly to the nice score and happy tone. Nudity can be eliminated.   MTI

Roberta (1933)   SNG, E, LK

There are few scores as good as Jerome Kern's music for this show ("Yesterdays," "Lovely to Look At," "I Won't Dance"), but the book is cumbersome, lengthy, and dated. Many sets, high-fashion clothes, cannot be contemporized. Some dance.   TW

Robert and Elizabeth (1965)   E, SNG, LK

This popular British musical, based on the romance of Elizabeth Barrett and Robert Browning, never made it to Broadway. It has a glorious score, strong singing-acting roles. Sets are simple, Victorian costuming expensive. Give it a try. Doesn't require much dance.   SF

The Rothschilds (1970)   M

    Episodic script about the banking family. Weak score. Nineteenth-century costumes, unit set. Little appeal, few women's roles, not much dance.   SF

Runaways (1978)   E, INT

    Young urban persons' show. Fair score; movement rather than dance, simplistic unit set, no unusual costuming.   SF

Salvation (1969)   E, INT

    Theme and music haven't aged well. Lacks audience appeal.   MTI

Say, Darling (1958)   E, INT

    Simple unit set, contemporary costumes, pleasant score. Amusing, low-key. Should be done more than it is.   TW

Seesaw (1973)   ST

    Touching, bittersweet musical with a nice score, some spirited dance numbers. Can be unit set; contemporary costumes.   SF

Seven Brides for Seven Brothers (1983)   E, D

    Stage version of 1950s movie hit has a pretty score and offers numerous roles for energetic young performers. Not easy to imagize. Strong dancing.   MTI

1776 (1968)   M

    Male-oriented production, unit set, eighteenth-century costumes. Nice, rousing score; patriotic appeal. Only two female roles. Choreographed movement rather than dance.   MTI

70, Girls, 70 (1971)   E, LK

    Fine show for older actors. Needs imagistic production; has nice score. Character dancing. Funny and topical.   SF

She Loves Me (1963)   SNG

    This tuneful, sentimental piece has had a recent comeback. Emphasis on song rather than dialogue; simple to imagize production. Don't try it without really good voices. Dancing is minimal.   TW

Shenandoah (1974)   SNG

    Rousing score, simple athletic dances. Civil War costumes, many sets. Another stage version of a movie, this musical lacks the outdoor ambiance necessary to the material.   SF

Showboat (1927)   SNG, E

    Elaborate sets and costumes, great score. Book is a major problem and black actors may not like the roles possible for them. Take a look at the MGM movie version on television for a more satisfying show.   RH

Side by Side by Sondheim (1977)   E, INT

Be inventive in the set, staging, and costuming with this history of Sondheim music. Great score. The cast can be expanded, but the show is intended for a small group.   MTI

Silk Stockings (1955)   ST, M, LK

Lots of sets necessary to this weak rendering of the film *Ninotchka*. Score is okay, but not top-drawer Cole Porter. Dances are few in this talky piece.   TW

Skyscraper (1965)   ST, M

Musical version of *Dream Girl* doesn't work. Weak score; fantasy interludes demand many sets and special effects.   SF

Snoopy (1983)   E, INT

This clever piece, with a finer score than *You're a Good Man, Charlie Brown*, was a west coast and touring success before it arrived in New York. In the meantime, it made a lot of hinterland audiences happy. Unit set, simple costumes. Young cast.   TW

Something's Afoot (1976)   INT, E

Only one set but full of technical gimmicks. Small cast; gentle spoof of Agatha Christie. Score is not exciting, but audiences like it.   SF

Song of Norway (1944)   SNG, E, CH

A beautiful, though difficult, score, and elaborate sets and costumes. Strong singers required; little dancing. The dreary movie revision has no relation to the stage play.   TW

The Sound of Music (1959)   W, CH

Has 1930s costumes; can be done in imagized production. Warm audience show. Overwritten. Little dance.   RH

South Pacific (1949)   M, SNG, CH

Heavy male cast, lots of sets, superb score, and great audience pleaser. Very little dance. 1940s military uniforms, nonimagistic production.   RH

Stop the World, I Want to Get Off (1962)   ST, W, INT

Fine score ("Someone Really Nice Like You," "What Kind of Fool Am I?") doesn't offset a weak and dated book. Imagistic production, circus costumes. Modified dance.   TW

Street Scene (1947)   SNG, LK, CH, E

Almost an opera, and based on the 1930s play about the citizens of a tenement block. That set is important to the environment of the characters, as are the 1930s clothes. Limited audience appeal; movement rather than dance.   RH

The Streets of New York (1963)   E, INT, LK

Gentle and appealing show based on the old nineteenth-century melodrama. Had a brief vogue; should be revived. Stylized set, mid-nineteenth-century costumes. Period dance.   SF

Sugar (1972)   ST, M

Musical of *Some Like It Hot* has a pretty good score, but can't cancel out vivid movie memories. Lots of sets; some intricate tap dance; 1930s costumes.   TW

Sweeney Todd (1979)   SNG, ST

Unit set, mid-nineteenth-century costumes. Very difficult score hasn't deterred productions, for it's already a huge hit with nonprofessional groups. Little dance; tone is bleak.   MTI

Sweet Charity (1966)   ST, D

A vehicle for the lead all the way. Lots of sets and no chance of stylizing the production. Great score, but strong dancers are a must, and the unhappy ending doesn't thrill audiences.   TW

Take Me Along (1959)   E, LK

Musical version of *Ah, Wilderness* rambles along. Though it starred Jackie Gleason, the script requires ensemble playing. Simple to imagize, early-twentieth-century costumes; not much dancing. Nice nostalgia piece.   TW

Tenderloin (1960)   E, LK

Late-nineteenth-century costumes and many elaborate sets. The script betrays its novel source, and a good score ("Artificial Flowers," "Gentle Young Johnny") and some strong dances can't help. Judicious pruning suggested.   TW

They're Playing Our Song (1978)   E, SNG, ST

Imagized setting requires slides and projections. The two leads need a great deal of charm. Movement rather than dance. Small chorus that cannot be expanded. Urban appeal only.   SF

Thirteen Daughters (1961)   W, LK

Strong possibilities for less-sophisticated groups of young people, but elaborate sets required for exotic locale. Weak score; few dances.   MTI

The Three-Penny Opera (1933)   E, SNG

Unit set, simple costuming, movement rather than dance. Popular, but on the seamy side. Great Kurt Weill score.   TW

Three Wishes for Jamie (1952)   M, LK

This bit of Irish whimsey is a good March bet. Many sets, turn-of-the-century costumes. Charming Irish dances, pretty score, verbose book.   SF

Tintypes (1980)   E, INT

One of the best of recent musicals. Good score of old favorites, unit set, and simple costumes. Crowd pleaser. Small cast, but can be slightly expanded.   MTI

Treemonisha (1975)   E, SNG
> Unusual musical capable of imagistic production. Offers strong roles for black actors. Good for community center production. Sometimes classified as an opera.   DPC

Two by Two (1970)   LK, INT, E
> Danny Kaye's hamming hampered the Broadway version, so this show hasn't been performed as much as it deserves. A fine score ("I Do Not Know a Day I Did Not Love You," "An Old Man") and a warm, audience-involving story. Two simple sets, easy costuming. Forget the projections; the show doesn't need them. Simple dances.   RH

Two Gentlemen of Verona (1971)   M, LK
> Rock music is dated. Unit set; simple costumes. Possible for young groups. Based on the Shakespeare play.   TW

The Unsinkable Molly Brown (1960)   ST, M
> Sprawls all over the place, through many sets and costume changes (early twentieth century). Strong woman's lead, and many tuneful numbers. A large-scale production.   MTI

Very Good Eddie (1915)   LK, E
> Charming trifle with few sets, and turn-of-the-century costuming. Pleasant score; some difficulty in casting the central characters because the plot depends on two couples, one unusually short and the other unusually tall.   TW

Via Galactica (1970)   E, LK
> Technically difficult futuristic show with weak score. Could use inventive, simple setting and costumes; might have youngster appeal.   SF

Walking Happy (1966)   M
> Dull musical version of a British play and movie. Score is weak; several sets, and late-Victorian costumes. Some dancing.   SF

West Side Story (1957)   D, SNG, E
> Young persons' musical with emphasis on dance (and demands strong dancers). Score full of hits. Material has not aged gracefully. Unit set, simple costumes. Good possibilities for black performers.   MTI

What Makes Sammy Run? (1964)   ST, SNG
> Unexciting musical about a Hollywood heel, has one semihit ("A Room without Windows") and a lot of sets.   TW

Where's Charley? (1968)   ST, M, LK
> Can be imagistic. Turn-of-the-century costumes, pretty score. Still hilarious, if you've got the man for the title role. Finale of Act I is a problem—a pokey ballet that goes nowhere.   MTI

Wildcat (1960)   ST, LK

Too often thought of as simply a star vehicle (Lucille Ball), this musical deserves more productions than it's been getting. Very fine score; some spirited dancing. Good for high school or community college. Lots of sets, including an oil well eruption; western costuming. Could be imagized.   TW

Wish You Were Here (1952)   E

You have to have a swimming pool, and, if you haven't, there's no reason for doing this overly ingenuous show.   MTI

The Wiz (1975)   E, D, SF

Easy, imagistic production, stylized costumes. Peppy show for black groups or mixed casts. Rousing audience response. Based on *The Wizard of Oz.*   SF

Wonderful Town (1953)   ST

Overwritten but still fun. Pretty score; can be more simply set than seems possible at first reading. Technical gimmicks can be simplified. Has 1930s costumes; little dance.   TW

Working (1978)   E

This loose adaptation of Studs Turkel's stories has caught on with younger groups. Uneven score; lots of energetic movement. Episodic structure, weak action line.   MTI

You're a Good Man, Charlie Brown (1967)   E, INT

Gentle and whimsical day with the "Peanuts" gang. Fun for the young crowd; oldsters often mistakenly classify it as strictly children's theatre.   TW

Your Own Thing (1967)   INT, E

Unit set; needs the projections for which the script calls. A blockbuster once, but its era is over. Might do as a nostalgia piece, but it's a little early to walk down memory lane into the late 1960s.   TW

Zorba (1968, 1983)   M, ST

Moribund version of the famed movie, which takes all the life force out of the original characters. Any show that suggests in its opening song that "Life is what you do while you're waiting to die" is not going to delight customers. Lots of sets and special effects (a mine cave-in) in spite of its claim to being an imagistic production.   SF

CHILDREN'S MUSICALS

Alice through the Looking Glass

Inexpensive, small-cast version with folk rock. Can be imaginatively costumed and set, and a sideline choral group can be used.   DPC

Androcles and the Lion
Flexible cast, unit set, simple costumes; allows audience interplay. Stylized dances.   PDS

Cinderella
Small-cast version of classic fairy tale. Adapts easily for touring. An excellent choice for newly formed production
groups.   CHP

The Emperor's New Clothes
Flexible cast, unit set, good dance possibilities, excellent score.
DPC

The Fabulous Fable Factory
Absolutely charming contemporary musical, can be all male,
all female, or a combination. Good audience interplay, minimal setting requirements, simple costumes. Strong movement
patterns. Easily adapted for touring.   DPC

The Feather Duster
Should be done with an elaborate production and costumes.
Highly magical and literate. Large cast.   DPC

Froggie Went a Courtin'
Good-sized cast, possibility of expansion. Unit set, animal costumes. Score needs to be kept up-tempo.   DPC

The Further Adventures of Maide Marian
Small cast with fine audience participation. Nice, sing-along
score. Simple set, costumes. Wonderful for female performers.
Swordplay possibilities.   DPC

The Genie of the Golden Key
Small cast, unit set, magical stage devices. Good use of audience. Simple costumes, dance can be expanded.   DPC

Jack and the Beanstalk
Cartoonlike version of the well-known tale. Small cast, peppy
score, medieval costumes suggestive of height differences. Tap
dance.   MTI

Kiddleywinks!
A clever show with a cast of three women and four men; extras
can be used. Ideal for grades four through eight. Imagistic set.
Many possibilities for clever dances; easy show to tour.   DPC

King Cole and the Country Witches
Unit set, small central cast, hordes of extras in nursery-rhyme
costumes. Sprightly score, special effects required. For tech-
nically proficient groups.   DPC

The Little Chimney Sweep
Large cast, elaborate costumes and set. Charming fantasy,
lackluster score.   PDS

The Magical Pied Piper

Middle-sized cast, one set, medieval costumes. Nice score and dance numbers highlight the ever-popular tale.   PDS

Mr. Herman and the Cave Company

Smallish cast, but wonderful for urban child groups. A good gimmick would be to get a well-known local disc jockey to tape the voices for the included radio broadcasts of the script. One set, simple costumes.   DPC

Peter Pan

Previously noted; can be pruned for younger casts. Technical wizardry necessary.   SF

Pinocchio

Nice version of the old tale. Unit set; requires good costuming and some special effects. Expand the dance. Nice score.   MTI

The Princess, the Poet and the Little Gray Man

Cast of ten can be expanded. Nice score. Good use of the audience, stylized dance. Simple set and costumes.   DPC

Showdown at the Sugarcane Saloon

A hilarious musical spoof of nineteenth-century melodramas, complete with many comic twists. A real hit with audiences of all ages. Music requires trained voices; works best with western set and costumes.   DPC

The Sleeping Beauty

Best of the versions, with an emphasis on comedy. Simple unit set and costumes. Good-sized cast, dance possibilities.   PDS

The Thirteen Clocks

Wonderful script and score, but needs elaborate sets and special costuming. Stylized movement rather than dance.   MTI

Tom Sawyer

A folk musical, nice score, simple sets and costumes, folk dance. On the long side for the very young, but the best version available.   MTI

Twelve Dancing Princesses

Far above other versions. Bouncy score, lots of dance, large cast, stylized sets and costumes.   DPC

The Velveteen Rabbit

Charming music and stylized movement enliven this wistful tale of beloved toys. Flexible cast, animal costuming a must, minimal set requirements.   DPC

Winnie the Pooh

Easy music, simple dance, flexible cast. Unit set, but imaginative costuming a must.   DPC

Young Andy Jackson
Small cast, more males than females. Unit set, simple costuming. Peppy music and folk dance possibilities in this good and unusual piece. DPC

YOUNG PERSONS' MUSICALS

Annabelle Broom, the Unhappy Witch
Great fun, tuneful, highly active, with a danced broomstick chase involving the audience. Really good bet. MTI

Babes in Arms
Previously noted; prune it. TW

Celebration
Previously noted. SF

Cinderella
Stage piece based on the 1957 television special. Charming score, more ensemble dance than in most children's shows. Needs elaborate sets and special effects as well as expensive costuming. For affluent groups only. RH

Cindy
Previously noted. TW

Drat! The Cat
Previously noted. SF

The Fabulous Fable Factory
Previously noted. DPC

The Hobbit
Large cast, unit set, imaginative costumes, some dance. Good version of the popular tale, greatly simplified. DPC

Legend of the Sun Child
An unusual show based on American Indian legend. Introduces subject of death to a young audience in a touching manner. Lends itself to an imagistic setting. Sophisticated musical score requires trained voices. Indian costumes needed. DPC

Little Women
Nice period score in the ever-popular tale of the beloved March family. Simple set, Civil War costumes. SF

Meet Me in St. Louis
Wonderful score. Pretty sets and turn-of-the-century costumes required, for the charm of the piece depends on having "the right look." Simple dances. TW

Melissa and the Magic Nutcracker
Probably the best of the Christmas musicals. Fine dance interludes help create an understanding of the spirit of Christmas as evidenced in foreign lands. Period costumes (1880) and stylized

fantasy costumes with international flavor. Small singing and acting cast, dancers flexible. Good choreography required. A "can't miss" money-maker.   DPC

Mr. Herman and the Cave Company
Previously noted.   DPC

Once upon a Mattress
Previously noted. Some reworking of the lines may be necessary, as well as the elimination of the queen's lover. Easy to suggest that Larkin and Harry were secretly married "away from the kingdom," and, thus, are happily expecting.   MTI

Peter Pan
Previously noted. No reason a teenaged boy can't play Peter instead of the usual female.   SF

Rock-n-Roll
Simple sets and costumes and a perky nostalgic score make this 1950s satire a good choice for teenagers. Period dances. Large cast.   PPC

Seven Brides for Seven Brothers
Previously noted.   MTI

Seventeen
Gentle score, lots of sets, turn-of-the-century costumes, large cast. Flavorsome tale, but the heroine has always been hard to take, and there isn't much excitement for contemporary youngsters.   SF

Snoopy
Previously noted.   TW

The Thirteen Clocks
Previously noted.   MTI

Tom Sawyer
Previously noted. Well-suited to this age group.   MTI

Via Galactica
Youngsters might have a good time with this space-age show after it's been cleaned up a bit.   SF

The Wizard of Oz
Familiar music, stylized dance. Large cast requires elaborate costuming. Lots of sets and tricky special effects.   TW

You're a Good Man, Charlie Brown
Previously noted.   TW

ZAS!
A bilingual musical comedy that deals with the working class in the United States. Animal characters; an excellent combination of teaching and entertaining.   CHP

RETIRED PERSONS' MUSICALS

Ain't Supposed to Die a Natural Death
> Previously noted.   SF

Anyone Can Whistle
> Previously noted.   MTI

Canterbury Tales
> Previously noted.   MTI

Dear World
> Previously noted.   MTI

The Education of H*Y*M*A*N K*A*P*L*A*N
> Previously noted.   SF

A Family Affair
> Previously noted.   MTI

Fanny
> Previously noted.   TW

The Fantasticks
> Previously noted.   MTI

Fiddler on the Roof
> Previously noted.   MTI

Follies
> Previously noted.   MTI

Gigi
> Previously noted.   TW

The Grass Harp
> Previously noted.   SF

Guys and Dolls
> Previously noted.   MTI

Li'l Abner
> Previously noted.   TW

Milk and Honey
> Previously noted.   TW

Mr. Wonderful
> Previously noted.   MTI

The Most Happy Fella
> Previously noted.   MTI

No, No, Nanette
> Previously noted.   TW

Salad Days (1965)   E, LK
> Charming, wistful, "very British" score and plot. Simple sets
> and costumes, little dance.   TW

1776
> Previously noted.   MTI

70, Girls, 70
> Previously noted.   SF

The Wizard of Oz
> Previously noted.   TW

3

PRODUCTION SOURCES

Included in this chapter are the current mailing addresses and telephone numbers of sources for information, materials, and supplies related to musical production. Production control organizations are listed alphabetically. The letters in parentheses following the name of each organization, are the abbreviation of the organization's name as used in earlier chapters. Other sources, for costumes, lighting, makeup, properties, scenery, and sound, are listed alphabetically under states, and for Canada and Puerto Rico. There has been no attempt to list every available source; rather, the list reflects a wide geographical distribution. Other sources can be found in *Simon's Directory* (see Bibliography) and in *Theatre Crafts* magazine, which is available in most educational libraries.

PRODUCTION CONTROL ORGANIZATIONS

Anchorage Press (A)
P.O. Box 8067
New Orleans, Louisiana 70182
(504) 283-8868

Baker's Plays (BP)
100 Chauncy Street
Boston, Massachusetts 02111
(617) 482-1280

Coach House Press (CHP)
53 West Jackson Boulevard
Chicago, Illinois 60604
(312) 922-8993

The Dramatic Publishing Company
(DPC)
4150 North Milwaukee Avenue
Chicago, Illinois 60641
(312) 545-2062

Music Theatre International (MTI)
1350 Avenue of the Americas
New York, New York 10019
(212) 975-6841

Performance Publishing Company
(PPC)
978 North McLean Boulevard
Elgin, Illinois 60120
(312) 697-5636

Pioneer Drama Service (PDS)
2172 South Colorado Boulevard
P.O. Box 22555
Denver, Colorado 80222
(303) 759-4297

The Rodgers and Hammerstein
Library (RH)
  Department S
  598 Madison Avenue
  New York, New York 10022
  (212) 486-0643

Samuel French (SF)
  25 West Forty-fifth Street
  New York, New York 10036
  (212) 382-0800

Tams-Witmark Music Library (TW)
  560 Lexington Avenue
  New York, New York 10022
  (212) 688-2525 or (800) 221-7196

COSTUME, FABRIC, AND ACCESSORIES SOURCES

Alabama

Andades Costume House
  260 South Broad Street
  Mobile, Alabama 36603
  (205) 433-5655

Blue Mountain Industries
  20 Blue Mountain Road
  Blue Mountain, Alabama 36201
  (205) 237-9461

Alaska

Dooley's
  1076 West Fireweed Lane
  Anchorage, Alaska 99503
  (907) 277-2811

Arizona

Mardi Gras Costume
  7341 Sixth Avenue
  Scottsdale, Arizona 85251
  (602) 946-4686

Arkansas

Daniels House of Costumes
  623 Beachwood Street
  Little Rock, Arkansas 72205
  (501) 664-2542

California

Act One Costume
  1530 MacArthur Boulevard
  Oakland, California 94602
  (415) 530-4141

Center Theatre Group Costume
Shop
  2101 Effie Street
  Los Angeles, California 90026
  (213) 662-2119

Norcostco
  2101 West Garvey Avenue North
  West Covina, California 91790
  (213) 960-4711

The Theatre Company
  633 North Benson Avenue
  Upland, California 91786
  (714) 982-5736

Colorado

Colorado Costume
  2100 Broadway
  Denver, Colorado 80205
  (303) 825-6874

Connecticut

Fierberg's
71 Church Street
Hartford, Connecticut 06103
(203) 247-1634

Delaware

"The Jester" Costumers
2604 Philadelphia Pike
Claymont, Delaware 19703
(302) 792-1883

District of Columbia

Costume Studio
35 Eighth Street NE
Washington, D.C. 20002
(202) 544-5843

Florida

Algy Costume and Uniform
P.O. Box 090490
440 Northeast First Avenue
Hallandale, Florida 33009
(305) 457-8100

Costume World
1301 West Copans Road
Pompano Beach, Florida 33064
(305) 974-2040 or (800) 327-4999

Star Styled
487 Northwest Forty-second
Avenue
Miami, Florida 33126
(305) 649-3030

Georgia

Costume Crafters
2979 Peachtree Street NE
Atlanta, Georgia 30305
(404) 237-8641

Jen-Nor Dancewear
4022 Cody Road
University Plaza
Columbus, Georgia 31907
(404) 563-6326

Norcostco
2089 Monroe Drive NE
Atlanta, Georgia 30324
(404) 874-7511

Hawaii

J. J. Productions of Hawaii
Ala Moana Building, Suite 1117
1441 Kapiolani Boulevard
Honolulu, Hawaii 96814
(808) 947-6871

Idaho

Fantasia Costumes
710 Orchard Street
Boise, Idaho 73705
(208) 344-3844

Illinois

Broadway Costumes
932 West Washington Boulevard
Chicago, Illinois 60607
(312) 829-6400

Chicago Costume Company
725 West Wrightwood
Chicago, Illinois 60614
(312) 528-1264

Josie Okain Costume and Theatre
Shop
2713 West Jefferson Street
Joliet, Illinois 60435
(815) 741-9303

Indiana

Landes Costume Company
811 North Capitol Avenue
Indianapolis, Indiana 46204
(317) 635-3655

Iowa

Globe Theatrical Supply
813 Pearl
Sioux City, Iowa 51101
(712) 255-0972

Kansas

Theatrical Services
128 South Washington
Wichita, Kansas 67202
(316) 263-4415

Kentucky

A. Baer Company
515 East Market Street
Louisville, Kentucky 40202
(502) 583-5521

Theatre House
P.O. Box 2090
400 West Third Street
Covington, Kentucky 41012
(606) 431-2414

Louisiana

Costume Headquarters
3634 Banks Street
New Orleans, Louisiana 70119
(504) 488-9523

Wards Costume Fabrics
2866 Government Street
Baton Rouge, Louisiana 70806
(504) 343-3371

Maine

Drapeau's Costumer
500 Lisbon
Lewiston, Maine 04240
(207) 782-7892

Maryland

Kinetic Artistry
7216 Carroll Avenue
Takoma Park, Maryland 20912
(301) 270-6666

Massachusetts

A and M Supply Company
240 Bedford Street
Lexington, Massachusetts 02173
(617) 862-5615

Hooker-Howe Costume Company
46-52 South Main Street
Bradford District
Haverhill, Massachusetts 01830
(617) 373-3731

Tracy Costumes
63 Melcher Street
Boston, Massachusetts 02210
(617) 542-9100

Michigan

Michigan Scenic and Stage
Equipment
410 North River
Ypsilanti, Michigan 48197
(313) 484-1395

Past Patterns
2017 Eastern SE
Grand Rapids, Michigan 49507
(616) 245-9456

Minnesota

Norcostco
   3203 North Highway 100
   Minneapolis, Minnesota 55422
   (612) 533-2791

Mississippi

Bright Image
   208 Commerce Street
   Jackson, Mississippi 39201
   (601) 352-5107

Missouri

Act One Creations
   1201 South Florence
   Springfield, Missouri 65807
   (417) 865-3278

Associated Theatrical Contractors
   307 West Eightieth Street
   Kansas City, Missouri 64114
   (816) 523-1655

Montana

Northwestern Costume Shop
   304 Short Street
   Missoula, Montana 59801
   (406) 549-2088

Nebraska

Theatrical Costumiers
   3140 Curning Street
   Omaha, Nebraska 68131
   (402) 346-8468

Nevada

Williams Costume Company
   1226 South Third Street
   Las Vegas, Nevada 89104
   (702) 384-1384

New Hampshire

The Costume Box
   814 Elm Street
   Manchester, New Hampshire
   03101
   (603) 623-8347

New Jersey

Kimberly Theatrics
   98 Line Road
   Trenton, New Jersey 08690
   (609) 587-7927

Norcostco
   375 Route 10
   Whippany, New Jersey 07981
   (201) 428-1177

New Mexico

The Costume House
   8200½ Menaul NE
   Albuquerque, New Mexico 87110
   (505) 294-4808

New York

A and J Distributors
   22 Northampton Street
   Buffalo, New York 14209
   (716) 886-7330

Animal Outfits for People
   P.O. Box 196
   Times Square Station
   New York, New York 10108
   (212) 840-6219

Costume Armour
   Shore Road
   P.O. Box 325
   Cornwall-on-Hudson, New York
   12520
   (914) 534-9120

Eaves Brooks Costume Company
2107 Forty-first Avenue
Long Island City, New York
11101
(212) 729-1010

North Carolina

Bob Whitaker Costumes
334 Cross Creek Mall
Fayetteville, North Carolina
28303
(919) 864-3765

Hinshaw's Mill Outlet
3200 Alamance Road, NC 62
Burlington, North Carolina
27215
(919) 226-1561

North Dakota

Kopelman Costume
512 First Avenue North
Fargo, North Dakota 58102
(701) 232-8729

Ohio

Masters Costumes
303 Federal Plaza West
Youngstown, Ohio 44503
(216) 744-2571

The Wright Place
143 East Main Street
Columbus, Ohio 43215
(614) 228-0550

Oklahoma

Hecklers
4034 North MacArthur
Oklahoma City, Oklahoma 73122
(405) 787-8603

Oregon

Hollywood Portland Costumers
522 Southwest Third Avenue
Portland, Oregon 97204
(503) 227-1582

Pennsylvania

Costumes Unlimited
1031 Forbes Avenue
Pittsburgh, Pennsylvania 15219
(412) 281-3277

Loeb Costume Collection
Millersville State College
Tanger Hall
Millersville, Pennsylvania 17551
(717) 872-3767

Meyers Costume Shoppe
4213 Kutztown Road
Temple, Pennsylvania 19560
(215) 929-0991

Rhode Island

Peko Creations
390 Pine Street
Pawtucket, Rhode Island 02860
(401) 722-6661

South Carolina

Costume Associates
701 East McBee
Greenville, South Carolina 29601
(801) 271-4260

South Dakota

Dakota Costume
221 North Dakota Street
Sioux Falls, South Dakota 57102
(605) 332-4012

Tennessee

Theatrical Equipment Rental
P.O. Box 3368
2040 Magnolia Avenue
Knoxville, Tennessee 37917
(615) 546-2082

Texas

Norcostco
2125 North Harwood Street
Dallas, Texas 75201
(214) 748-4581

Performing Arts Supply Company
10161 Harwin, Suite 115
Houston, Texas 77036
(713) 776-8900

Southern Importers
4825 San Jacinto Street
Houston, Texas 77004
(713) 524-8236

Utah

Salt Lake City Costume
1701 South 11E Street
Salt Lake City, Utah 84106
(801) 467-9494

Virginia

Stein's Capezio Dance-Theatre
Shop
1180 North Highland Street
Arlington, Virginia 22201
(703) 522-2661

Washington

Brockland
901 Olive Way
Seattle, Washington 98101
(206) 682-5898

Cerulean Blue
P.O. Box 21168
Seattle, Washington 98111
(206) 625-9647

West Virginia

The Body Shop
405 High Street
Morgantown, West Virginia
26505
(304) 296-9795

Wisconsin

Creative Services International
218 West Walnut
Milwaukee, Wisconsin 53212
(414) 265-3377

Canada

Ace Novelties
1212 Commercial Drive
Vancouver, British Columbia
V5L2M9 Canada
(604) 255-2661

Joseph Ponton (Costumes)
451 Saint Sulpice
Montreal, Quebec H2Y2V9
Canada
(514) 849-3238

Malabar
14 McCaul Street
Toronto, Ontario M5T1V6
Canada
(416) 598-2581

Mallabar
375 Hargrave Street
Winnipeg, Manitoba R3B2K2
Canada
(204) 943-4506

Puerto Rico

Wardrobe Research and Design
904 Ponce de Leon Avenue
Miramar
San Juan, Puerto Rico 00907
(809) 722-3023

LIGHTING SOURCES

Alabama

Hammond Industries
8000 Madison Pike
Madison, Alabama 35758
(205) 772-9626

Alaska

Alaska Stagecrafts
P.O. Box 4-2665
1025 Orca Street, Number S-7
Anchorage, Alaska 99509
(907) 276-5671

Arizona

Centerline Stage and Studio
Lighting
947 South Forty-eighth Street,
Number 123
Tempe, Arizona 85281
(602) 967-5321

California

Angstrom Stage Lighting
7049 Vineland
North Hollywood, California
91605
(213) 764-6858

Birns and Sawyer
1026 North Highland Avenue
Hollywood, California 90038
(213) 466-8211

Olesen
1535 Ivar Avenue
Hollywood, California 90028
(213) 461-4631

Strand Century
P.O. Box 9004
18111 South Santa Fe Avenue
Rancho Dominguez, California
90224
(213) 637-7500

Colorado

Productions Unlimited
3128 Morris
Pueblo, Colorado 81008
(303) 545-5369

Connecticut

LSS Laboratories
473 Washington Avenue
North Haven, Connecticut 06473
(203) 239-2605

District of Columbia

City Lights
1232 Ninth Street NW
Washington, D.C. 20001
(202) 289-1090

Florida

Apollo Lights and Sound
  1950 East Fourth Avenue
  Hialeah, Florida 33010
  (305) 887-8899

Bay Stage Lighting Company
  310 South MacDill Avenue
  Tampa, Florida 33609
  (813) 877-1089

Georgia

Lighting and Production
Equipment
  750 Ralph McGill Boulevard
  Atlanta, Georgia 30312
  (404) 681-0130

Norcostco
  2089 Monroe Drive NE
  Atlanta, Georgia 30324
  (404) 874-7511

Stage Front Lighting
  528 Indian Street
  Savannah, Georgia 31401
  (912) 236-1345

Strand Century
  950 Hemingway Road
  Stone Mountain, Georgia 30088
  (404) 469-8468

Theatre Production Service
  3519 Chamblee-Dunwoody Road
  Atlanta, Georgia 30341
  (404) 452-8700 or (800) 241-8700

Illinois

ESV
  525 Court Street
  Pekin, Illinois 61554
  (309) 347-6685

Hub Electric Company
  6207 Commercial Road
  Crystal Lake, Illinois 60014
  (312) 530-6860

Major Control Products
  740 Industrial Drive
  Cary, Illinois 60013
  (312) 639-8200

Strand Century
  323 Park Lane
  Lake Bluff, Illinois 60044
  (312) 234-5547

Indiana

Indianapolis State Sales and Rentals
  905 Massachusetts Avenue
  Indianapolis, Indiana 46202
  (317) 635-9430

Mix International Lighting
  1120 Meigs Avenue
  Jeffersonville, Indiana 47130
  (812) 283-7901

Iowa

Rose's Theatrical Supply
  1682 Northwest 109th
  Des Moines, Iowa 50322
  (515) 225-0714

Kentucky

General Lighting Products
  817 Nandino Boulevard
  Lexington, Kentucky 40511
  (606) 252-5664 or (800) 354-9079

Louisiana

American Electric and Display
Company
  640 Frenchmen Street
  New Orleans, Louisiana 70116
  (504) 944-0314

Maine

Maine Lighting Company
  P.O. Box 152
  Route 24
  Bowdoinham, Maine 04008
  (207) 666-3246

Maryland

Baltimore Stage Lighting
  4109 Aquarium Place
  Baltimore, Maryland 21215
  (301) 358-2330

Hal's Stage Lighting
  3500 Parkdale Avenue
  Baltimore, Maryland 21211
  (301) 462-2444

Massachusetts

Adams Lighting Company
  12 Beacon Street
  Somerville, Massachusetts 02143
  (617) 492-6363

BWA Lighting Company
  349 Nichols Street
  Norwood, Massachusetts 02062
  (617) 769-0908

Limelight Productions
  P.O. Box 816
  Yale Hall
  Stockbridge, Massachusetts
  01262
  (413) 298-3771

Michigan

Fantasee Lighting
  404 North River
  Ypsilanti, Michigan 48197
  (313) 482-6565

Master Stage Lighting
  21660 Grand River
  Detroit, Michigan 48219
  (313) 531-8895

Minnesota

Gopher Stage Lighting
  2839 Eleventh Avenue South
  Minneapolis, Minnesota 55407
  (612) 871-0138

Missouri

Associated Theatrical Contractors
  307 West Eightieth Street
  Kansas City, Missouri 64114
  (816) 523-1655

Mega Products
  2671 McKelvey Road
  Saint Louis, Missouri 63043
  (314) 291-7618

Nebraska

Slipper Theatre Supply
  1502 Davenport Street
  Omaha, Nebraska 68102
  (402) 341-5715

Nevada

Lighting Dynamics
  5325 South Valley View Street
  Las Vegas, Nevada 89118
  (702) 736-3824

New Jersey

Atlantic City State Lighting
Company
32 Old Turnpike
Pleasantville, New Jersey 08232
(609) 641-8447

New Mexico

Young Sales
1100 Turner Drive NE
Albuquerque, New Mexico 87123
(505) 293-8032

New York

Alcone Company
578 Eighth Avenue
New York, New York 10018
(212) 594-3980

American Stage Lighting Company
1331C North Avenue
New Rochelle, New York 10804
(914) 636-5538

Theatre Production Service
26 South Highland Avenue
Ossining, New York 10562
(914) 941-0367

North Carolina

Alpha Sound and Light
1842 Freedom Drive
Charlotte, North Carolina 28208
(704) 376-1655

Dudley Theatrical Equipment
P.O. Box 551
4925 Harley Drive
Walkertown, North Carolina
27051
(919) 595-2122

Omni Stage and Lighting
Equipment Company
P.O. Box 2249
Raleigh, North Carolina 27602
(919) 833-7469 or (800) 334-8353

Ohio

Best Devices Company
10921 Briggs Road
Cleveland, Ohio 44111
(216) 941-5589

ETA Lighting
1710 Enterprise Parkway
Twinsburg, Ohio 44087
(216) 425-3388

Oklahoma

B-W Lighting System
P.O. Box 45162
7610 East Forty-sixth Street
Tulsa, Oklahoma 74147
(918) 664-1111

Oregon

Andromeda Lighting
838 Bennett, Suite 5
Medford, Oregon 97501
(503) 779-7488

Electronics Diversified
1675 Northwest 216th Street
Hillsboro, Oregon 97123
(503) 645-5533

Pennsylvania

Community Light and Sound
333 East Fifth Street
Chester, Pennsylvania 19013
(215) 876-3400 or (800) 523-4934

McManus Enterprises
111 Union Avenue
Bala Cynwyd, Pennsylvania
19004
(215) 664-8600 or (800) 523-0348

South Carolina

Dixie Electronics
500 Pendleton Street
Greenville, South Carolina 29601
(803) 232-5357

Southern Lites
1720 Batallion Drive
Charleston, South Carolina 29412
(803) 795-9517

Tennessee

Interstate Theatrical Lighting and
Supply
1421 Fourth Avenue South
Nashville, Tennessee 37210
(615) 259-4696

Texas

Dallas Stage Lighting and
Equipment Company
2813 Florence
Dallas, Texas 75204
(214) 827-9380

Utah

Electro Controls
2975 South 300 West
Salt Lake City, Utah 84115
(801) 487-9861

General Theatrical Supply
2153 South 700 East
Salt Lake City, Utah 84106
(801) 485-5012

Virginia

Backstage
310 West Broad Street
Richmond, Virginia 23220
(804) 644-1433

Scene Tech Entertainment Lighting
and Sound
P.O. Box 4488
Alexandria, Virginia 22303
(703) 960-8696

Washington

Clear Light Systems Company
608 Nineteenth East
Seattle, Washington 98112
(206) 322-8811

West Virginia

Imperial Display
1057 Main Street
Wheeling, West Virginia 26003
(304) 233-0711

Wisconsin

Electronic Theatre Controls
3002 West Beltline Highway
Middleton, Wisconsin 53562
(608) 831-4116

NSC Systems Company
P.O. Box 320
1615 Washington Street
Two Rivers, Wisconsin 54241
(414) 684-3650

Canada

CA Creative Lighting
3208 Beta Avenue
Burnaby, British Columbia
V5G4K4 Canada
(604) 294-1266

Canadian Staging Products
571 Adelaide Street East
Toronto, Ontario M5A1N8
Canada
(416) 947-9400

MAKEUP AND WIG SOURCES

California

Cabaret Costume
1302 Kingsdale Avenue
Redondo Beach, California 90277
(213) 370-0098

California Theatrical Supply
747 Polk Street
San Francisco, California 94109
(415) 928-5824

Delaware

"The Jester" Costumes
2604 Philadelphia Pike
Claymont, Delaware 19703
(302) 792-1883

District of Columbia

Backstage
2101 P Street NW
Washington, D.C. 20037
(202) 775-1488

Georgia

Norcostco
2089 Monroe Drive NE
Atlanta, Georgia 30324
(404) 874-7511

Illinois

Chicago Hair Goods Company
428 South Wabash Avenue
Chicago, Illinois 60605
(312) 427-8600

Indiana

Landes Costume Company
811 North Capitol Avenue
Indianapolis, Indiana 46204
(317) 635-3655

Iowa

Globe Theatrical Supply
813 Pearl
Sioux City, Iowa 51101
(712) 255-0972

Rose's Theatrical Supply
1682 North West 109th Street
Des Moines, Iowa 50322
(515) 225-0714

Kansas

Kansas City Costume Company
8125 Santa Fe
Overland Park, Kansas 66204
(913) 642-5025

Kentucky

Theatre House
P.O. Box 2090
400 West Third Street
Covington, Kentucky 41012
(606) 431-2414

Massachusetts

The Make-Up Place
100 Boylston Street, Suite 828
Boston, Massachusetts 02116
(617) 542-8138

Mississippi

Bright Image
208 Commerce Street
Jackson, Mississippi 39201
(601) 352-5107

New Hampshire

Mikan Theatricals
54 Tide Mill Road
Hampton, New Hampshire 03842
(603) 926-2744

New Mexico

The Costume House
8200½ Menaul NE
Albuquerque, New Mexico 87110
(505) 294-4808

New York

Alcone Company
575 Eighth Avenue
New York, New York 10018
(212) 594-3980

Bob Kelly Cosmetics
151 West Forty-sixth Street
New York, New York 10036
(212) 819-0030

Mehron
250 West Fortieth Street
New York, New York 10018
(212) 997-1011

M. Stein Theatrical Makeup
430 Broome Street
New York, New York 10013
(212) 226-2430

North Carolina

Bob Whitaker Costumes
334 Cross Creek Mall
Fayetteville, North Carolina
28303
(919) 864-3765

Morris Costumes and Theatrical
Supplies
3108 Monroe Road
Charlotte, North Carolina 28205
(704) 333-0004

Standard Theatre Supply Company
P.O. Box 20660
125 Higgins Street
Greensboro, North Carolina
27420
(919) 272-6165

Ohio

Krause Costume Company
2439 Superior Avenue
Cleveland, Ohio 44114
(216) 241-6466

The Wright Place
143 East Main Street
Columbus, Ohio 43215
(614) 228-0550

Oklahoma

Heckler's
4034 North MacArthur
Oklahoma City, Oklahoma 73122
(405) 787-8603

Pennsylvania

Baum's
106-114 South Eleventh Street
Philadelphia, Pennsylvania 19107
(215) 923-2244

Meyer's Costume Shoppe
4213 Kutztown Road
Temple, Pennsylvania 19560
(215) 929-0991

Texas

Performing Arts Supply Company
10161 Harwin, Suite 115
Houston, Texas 77036
(713) 776-8900

Canada

Ace Novelties
1212 Commercial Drive
Vancouver, British Columbia
V5L2M9
Canada
(604) 255-2661

Mallabar
375 Hargrave Street
Winnipeg, Manitoba R3B2K2
Canada
(204) 943-4506

PROPERTY SOURCES

Arizona

American Fiberglass
701 North Twenty-second Avenue
Phoenix, Arizona 85009
(602) 257-0521

J. R. Russell Systems
1045 East Camelback Road
Phoenix, Arizona 85014
(602) 266-6918

California

American Scenery
18555 Eddy Street
Northridge, California 91324
(213) 886-1585

The Hand Prop Room
5700 Venice Boulevard
Los Angeles, California 90019
(213) 931-1534

Connecticut

Stagerite Associates
P.O. Box 8653
New Haven, Connecticut 06531
(203) 271-0502

District of Columbia

Backstage
2101 P Street NW
Washington, D.C. 20037
(202) 775-1488

Georgia

Herschel Harrington Studio
132 Tenth Street NE
Atlanta, Georgia 30309
(404) 892-0065

Hawaii

Brady Photo
741 A. Kelikoi Street
Honolulu, Hawaii 06813
(808) 537-9364

Illinois

Josie Okain Costume and Theatre
Shop
2713 West Jefferson Street
Joliet, Illinois 60435
(815) 741-9303

Stagecraft
312 North Laflin
Chicago, Illinois 60607
(312) 243-5317

Maryland

Fitzhugh and Thomas
P.O. Box 3148
Baltimore, Maryland 21228
(301) 747-5589

Massachusetts

BN Productions
123 Forest Street
Saugus, Massachusetts 01906
(617) 233-4524

Missouri

Kennark Productions
30 West Pershing Road, Number
25
Kansas City, Missouri 64108
(816) 474-8024

SECT Theatrical Supply
406 East Eighteenth Street
Kansas City, Missouri 64108
(816) 471-1239

New Mexico

The Costume House
8200½ Menaul NE
Albuquerque, New Mexico
87110
(505) 294-4808

North Carolina

North Carolina Scenic Studios
187 Waughtown Street
Winston-Salem, North Carolina
27107
(919) 761-2123

Ohio

Schell Scenic Studio
841 South Front Street
Columbus, Ohio 43206
(614) 444-9550

Pennsylvania

Frank E. Davis Associates
630 New York Avenue
Rochester, Pennsylvania 15074
(412) 774-2133

Texas

Austin Theatrical Supply
  1100 East Fifth Street
  Austin, Texas 78702
  (512) 472-8043

Virginia

Scene Tech Entertainment Lighting
and Sound
  P.O. Box 4488
  Alexandria, Virginia 22303
  (703) 960-8686

Washington

Brockland
  901 Olive Way
  Seattle, Washington 98101
  (206) 682-5898

West Virginia

Theatre Arts Studio
  847-51 Plutus Avenue
  Chester, West Virginia 26034
  (304) 387-3796

Canada

Addmore Equipment
  3814 Victoria Park Avenue
  Willowdale, Ontario M2H3H7
  Canada
  (416) 494-5882

SCENERY EQUIPMENT AND SUPPLY SOURCES

Alaska

Alaska Stagecrafts
  P.O. Box 4-2665
  1025 Orca Street, Number S-7
  Anchorage, Alaska 99509
  (907) 276-5671

Arizona

J. R. Russell Systems
  1045 East Camelback Road
  Phoenix, Arizona 85014
  (602) 266-6918

California

Center Theatre Group Costume
Shop
  2101 Effie Street
  Los Angeles, California 90026
  (213) 662-2119

Grosh Scenic Studios
  4114 Sunset Boulevard
  Hollywood, California 90029
  (213) 662-1134

Musson Theatrical
  582 Stockton Avenue
  San Jose, California 95126
  (408) 298-0210

Olesen
  1535 Ivar Avenue
  Hollywood, California 90028
  (213) 461-4631

Colorado

Theatrix
  5138 East Thirty-ninth Avenue
  Denver, Colorado 80207
  (303) 388-9345

Connecticut

Stagerite Associates
P.O. Box 8653
New Haven, Connecticut 06531
(203) 271-0502

Delaware

Delaware Theatrical Supply
2 South Railroad Avenue
Wyoming, Delaware 19934
(302) 697-1709

Florida

Design Line
6204 Benjamin Road, Suite 209
Tampa, Florida 33614
(813) 886-5073

Miami Stagecraft
2855 East Eleventh Avenue
Hialeah, Florida 33013
(305) 836-9356

Georgia

Theatre Production Service
3519 Chamblee Dunwoody
Atlanta, Georgia 30341
(404) 452-8700 or (800) 241-8700

Hawaii

Brady Photo
741 A. Kelikoi Street
Honolulu, Hawaii 96813
(808) 537-9364

Illinois

Stagecraft
312 North Laflin
Chicago, Illinois 60607
(312) 243-5317

Indiana

Indianapolis Stage Sales and
Rentals
905 Massachusetts Avenue
Indianapolis, Indiana 46202
(317) 635-9430

Iowa

Globe Theatrical Supply
813 Pearl
Sioux City, Iowa 51101
(712) 255-0972

Louisiana

Moon Sound
4239 Banks Street
New Orleans, Louisiana 70119
(504) 486-5577

Maryland

Fitzhugh and Thomas
P.O. Box 3148
Baltimore, Maryland 21228
(301) 747-5589

Kinetic Artistry
7216 Carroll Avenue
Takoma Park, Maryland 20912
(301) 270-6666

Massachusetts

A and M Supply Company
240 Bedford Street
Lexington, Massachusetts 02173
(617) 862-5615

Charles H. Stewart and Company
P.O. Box 187
8 Clarendon Avenue
Somerville, Massachusetts 02144
(617) 625-2407

Michigan

Michigan Scenic and Stage
Equipment
410 North River
Ypsilanti, Michigan 48197
(313) 484-1395

Tobins Lake Studio
2650 Seven Mile Road
South Lyon, Michigan 48178
(313) 449-4444

Minnesota

Norcostco
3203 North Highway 100
Minneapolis, Minnesota 55422
(612) 533-2791

Theatrical Services and Consultants
9010 Pillsbury Avenue, South
Minneapolis, Minnesota 55420
(612) 884-2355

Mississippi

Bright Image
208 Commerce Street
Jackson, Mississippi 39201
(601) 352-5107

Missouri

Associated Drapery and Textile
Company
3226 Olive Street
Saint Louis, Missouri 63108
(314) 531-7222

Kenmark Productions
30 West Pershing Road,
Number 25
Kansas City, Missouri 64108
(816) 474-8024

SECT Theatrical Supply
406 East Eighteenth Street
Kansas City, Missouri 64108
(816) 471-1239

Nevada

Dick Ponts Gaffer Mobile
13735 Algonquin Drive
Reno, Nevada 89511
(702) 851-0202

New Hampshire

Mikan Theatricals
54 Tide Mill Road
Hampton, New Hampshire 03842
(603) 926-2744

New Jersey

Atlantic City Stage Lighting
Company
32 Old Turnpike
Pleasantville, New Jersey 08232
(609) 641-8447

New York

Alcone Company
575 Eighth Street
New York, New York 10018
(212) 594-3980

Bestek Equipment Supply
386 Newbridge Avenue
East Meadow, New York 11554
(516) 794-3953

Bruce Porter/Bruce Rayvid Stage
Scenery
155 Attorney Street
New York, New York 10002
(212) 460-5050

North Carolina

Atlantic Stage Equipment
1326 Central Avenue
Charlotte, North Carolina 28205
(704) 375-1438

Audio Unlimited of North America
P.O. Box 9225
11 Battleground Court
Greensboro, North Carolina
27408
(919) 274-4682

Omni Stage and Lighting
Equipment Company
P.O. Box 2249
Raleigh, North Carolina 27602
(919) 833-7469 or (800) 334-8353

Ohio

Schell Scenic Studio
841 South Front Street
Columbus, Ohio 43206
(614) 444-9550

Oklahoma

Oklahoma City Scenic Company
1223 North May Street
Oklahoma City, Oklahoma 73107
(405) 947-0118

Pennsylvania

Frank E. Davis Associates
630 New York Avenue
Rochester, Pennsylvania 15074
(412) 774-2133

M and M Lighting Company
P.O. Box 493
Route 447
East Stroudsburg, Pennsylvania
18301
(717) 424-5200

Tennessee

Interstate Theatrical Lighting and
Supply
1421 Fourth Avenue South
Nashville, Tennessee 37210
(615) 259-4696

Texas

Austin Theatrical Supply
1100 East Fifth Street
Austin, Texas 78702
(512) 472-8043

Guardian Packaging
3615 Security Street
Garland, Texas 75042
(214) 349-1500

Houston Stage Equipment
Corporation
2301 Dumble
Houston, Texas 77023
(713) 926-4441

Production Services
6016 G-3 Doniphan
El Paso, Texas 79932
(915) 584-6903

Utah

General Theatrical Supply
2153 South 700 East
Salt Lake City, Utah 84106
(801) 485-5012 or (801) 485-2732

Virginia

Backstage
310 West Broad Street
Richmond, Virginia 23220
(804) 644-1433

Scene Tech Entertainment Lighting
and Sound
   P.O. Box 4488
   Alexandria, Virginia 22303
   (703) 960-8686

Washington

Theatrical Resource and Supply
Cooperative
   1726 Commerce
   Tacoma, Washington 98402
   (206) 272-7289

West Virginia

Theatre Arts Studio
   847-51 Plutus Avenue
   Chester, West Virginia 26034
   (304) 387-3796

Wisconsin

Creative Services International
   218 West Walnut
   Milwaukee, Wisconsin 53212
   (414) 265-3377

Mainstage Theatrical Supply
   301 North Water Street
   Milwaukee, Wisconsin 53202
   (414) 278-0878

Canada

Michael Hagen
   1751 Richardson Street, 8th Floor
   Montreal, Quebec H3K1G6
   Canada
   (514) 931-6648 or (514) 697-7437

SOUND SOURCES

Alabama

Hammond Industries
   8000 Madison Pike
   Madison, Alabama 35758
   (205) 772-9626

Alaska

Alaska Stagecrafts
   P.O. Box 4-2665
   1025 Orca Street, Number S-7
   Anchorage, Alaska 99509
   (907) 276-5671

Arizona

J. R. Russell Systems
   1045 East Camelback Road
   Phoenix, Arizona 85014
   (602) 266-6918

Klipsch and Associates
   P.O. Box 688
   Hope, Arizona 71801
   (501) 777-6751

Arkansas

Bylites
   P.O. Box 3131
   1118 West Markham Street
   Little Rock, Arkansas 72203
   (501) 312-4535

California

Continental Sound and Acoustics
   26810-A Oak Avenue
   Canyon Country, California
   91351
   (805) 251-4206

Orban Associates
645 Bryant Street
San Francisco, California 94107
(415) 957-1067

Colorado

Productions Unlimited
3128 Morris
Pueblo, Colorado 81008
(303) 545-5369

Connecticut

AKG Acoustics
77 Selleck Street
Stamford, Connecticut 06902
(203) 348-2121

Delaware

Brandywine Sound Company
Route 82
Yorklyn, Delaware 19736
(302) 239-2101

Delaware Theatrical Supply
2 South Railroad Avenue
Wyoming, Delaware 19934
(302) 697-1709

Florida

Apollo Light and Sound
1950 East Fourth Avenue
Hialeah, Florida 33010
(305) 887-8899

Design Line
6204 Benjamin Road, Suite 209
Tampa, Florida 33614
(813) 886-5073

Georgia

Norcostco
2089 Monroe Drive NE
Atlanta, Georgia 30324
(404) 874-7511

Wil-Kin Theatre Supply
800 Lambert Drive
Atlanta, Georgia 30324
(404) 876-0347

Indiana

Crown International
1718 West Mishawaka Road
Elkhart, Indiana 46517
(219) 294-5571

Iowa

Globe Theatrical Supply
813 Pearl
Sioux City, Iowa 51101
(712) 255-0972

Kansas

Galaxy Audio
625 East Pawnee Street
Wichita, Kansas 67211
(316) 263-2852

Louisiana

Moon Sound
4239 Banks Street
New Orleans, Louisiana 70119
(504) 486-5577

Maryland

Auburn Sound Corporation
5308 Lanham Station Road
Lanham, Maryland 20706
(301) 459-1959

Massachusetts

The Bose Corporation
The Mountain
Framingham, Massachusetts
01701
(617) 879-7330

John F. Allen
64 Bowen Street
Newton Centre, Massachusetts
02159
(617) 244-1737

Michigan

Electro-Voice
600 Cecil Street
Buchanan, Michigan 49107
(616) 695-6831

Ringold Theatre Equipment
Company
6504 Twenty-eighth Street SE
Grand Rapids, Michigan 49506
(616) 957-2684

Missouri

Associated Theatrical Contractors
307 West Eightieth Street
Kansas City, Missouri 64114
(816) 523-1655

Mega Products
2671 McKelvey Road
St. Louis, Missouri 63043
(314) 291-7618

Nebraska

Slipper Theatre Supply
1502 Davenport Street
Omaha, Nebraska 68102
(402) 341-5715

Stanal Sound
816 East Twenty-fifth Street
Kearney, Nebraska 68847
(308) 237-2207

New Jersey

East Coast Lighting and Sound
Company
P.O. Box 385
700 Lawlins Road, Building 52
Wyckoff, New Jersey 07481
(201) 652-7641

New York

Communication Systems
215 Lexington Avenue
New York, New York 10016
(212) 481-6500

Posthorn Recordings
142 West Twenty-sixth Street,
10th Floor
New York, New York 10001
(212) 242-3737

Specialized Audio
Road 5
Route 50 and Hutchins Road
Saratoga Springs, New York
12866
(518) 885-8966

North Carolina

Alpha Sound and Light
1824 Freedom Drive
Charlotte, North Carolina 28208
(704) 376-1655

Dudley Theatrical Equipment
P.O. Box 551
4925 Harley Drive
Walkertown, North Carolina
27051
(919) 595-2122

Long Engineering Company
  961 Burke Street
  Winston-Salem, North Carolina
  27101
  (919) 725-2306

Omni Stage and Lighting Company
  P.O. Box 2249
  Raleigh, North Carolina 27602
  (919) 833-7469 or (800) 334-8353

Ohio

Audio-Technica U.S.
  1221 Commerce Drive
  Stow, Ohio 44224
  (216) 686-2600

Brite Lites
  4135 Westward Avenue
  Columbus, Ohio 43228
  (614) 272-1404

Oregon

Sunn Musical Equipment
Company
  19350 Southwest Eighty-ninth
  Avenue
  Tualatin, Oregon 97062
  (503) 638-6551

Pennsylvania

Community Light and Sound
  333 East Fifth Street
  Chester, Pennsylvania 19013
  (215) 876-3400 or (800) 523-4934

M & M Lighting Company
  P.O. Box 493
  Route 447
  East Stroudsburg, Pennsylvania
  18301
  (717) 424-5200

South Carolina

Custom Recording and Sound
  P.O. Box 7647
  1225 Pendleton Street
  Greenville, South Carolina 29610
  (803) 269-5018

Tennessee

Audiotronics
  P.O. Box 18838
  3750 Old Getwell Road
  Memphis, Tennessee 38118
  (901) 362-1350

Harrison Systems
  P.O. Box 22964
  Nashville, Tennessee 37202
  (615) 834-1184

Theatrical Equipment Rental
  P.O. Box 3368
  2040 Magnolia Avenue
  Knoxville, Tennessee 37917
  (615) 546-2082

Texas

CFA Media Specialties
  P.O. Box 34567
  8234 Vicar
  San Antonio, Texas 78233
  (512) 657-5997

Showco
  9011 Governors Row
  Dallas, Texas 75247
  (214) 630-1188

Utah

General Theatrical Supply
  2153 South 700 East
  Salt Lake City, Utah 84106
  (801) 485-5012 or (801) 485-2732

Virginia

Backstage
310 West Broad Street
Richmond, Virginia 23220
(804) 644-1433

Scene Tech Entertainment Lighting
and Sound
P.O. Box 4488
Alexandria, Virginia 22303
(703) 960-8686

Washington

Laser Concepts
3284 Eightieth Avenue SE
Mercer Island, Washington
98040
(206) 232-6256

Lighting Specialties
5001 Twenty-fifth Avenue NE
Seattle, Washington 98105
(206) 522-6594

West Virginia

Theatre Arts Studio
847-51 Plutus Avenue
Chester, West Virginia 26034
(304) 387-3796

Wisconsin

Full Compass Systems
6729 Seybold Road
Madison, Wisconsin 53719
(608) 271-1100 or (800) 356-5844

The Lighthouse
2800 Doe Trail
Green Bay, Wisconsin 54303
(414) 497-8314

Canada

Canadian Staging Projects
571 Adelaide Street East
Toronto, Ontario M5A1N8
Canada
(416) 947-9400

GLOSSARY

Broadside. A single-sheet program or advertising flyer.

Business. Action by an actor to help individualize a character, e.g., frequent pacing or rubbing together of hands to show nervousness.

Callback. A session following the initial auditions for those auditionees whom the director wishes to see and hear again before making final cast decisions.

Call-board. A prominently located bulletin board used for all major announcements from the director to the cast and crew.

Chamber theatre. A stylized performance using a narrator or narrators, with emphasis on ritualized movement, and with possible use of scripts by the narrators.

Combo. A small orchestra usually composed of piano, drums, bass, and perhaps a single brass or woodwind instrument.

Controlling organization. An agency from which the performance rights for a musical production are leased.

Cue-to-cue rehearsal. A rehearsal involving performers and orchestra; only musical numbers and dialogue that is underscored by music are performed. All other action is omitted.

Drop curtain. A curtain that can be brought in from the sides of, or from above, the playing area. This curtain serves as a scenic background and may or may not be painted.

Elevations. Scaled drawings of a designer's setting as seen from several angles.

Fingertipping. Giving line readings and exact gestures for actors to copy, as well as holding private consultations with the actors at which they learn to copy minute inflections in line readings.

Floor plan. Scaled blueprint of a scene design as seen from above; furniture and other set props are indicated, as well as all entrances and exits.

Fly gallery. A scenery-shifting system set above a stage.

Focus. The placement of actors in relation to the stage setting so that the audience's attention is channeled to the appropriate onstage locations.

Follow spotlight. A large, portable spotlight mounted on a stand and operated by a lighting technician. The beam of this light can be directed on a single performer or on a small group, and can follow the performers' movements on the stage.

French scene. A subdivision of a scene for rehearsal purposes. The subdivision is determined by entrances and exits of selected characters. For example, a French scene may begin with the entrance of character A and continue until either character B enters or another character on stage exits.

Gobo. An extension on a spotlight that gives a specific shape to the beam of light.

Imagistic set. A nonrealistic, composite stage setting emphasizing design through suggestion rather than through realistic detail.

Libretto. A book of dialogue and song lyrics.

Masking. Curtains or scenery designed to hide backstage areas from the audience's view.

Model. A scaled miniature of the stage setting, including set properties and furnishings.

Optimum space. Maximum use by the director of available playing areas for character placement and movements.

Pace rehearsal. A rehearsal at which the dialogue and song lyrics are carefully articulated, but at a rapid speed. Musical tempo likewise is increased. Actors pick up cues three words earlier than usual.

Pantomime. Action without words.

Playing areas. Divisions of the performance area in which the action is played.

Production contract. A legal document granting performance rights and stipulating restrictions.

Properties. Objects used onstage in a performance. These objects, or properties, can be divided into the following five categories:

1. Hand props—objects carried onto the stage and handled by an actor;
2. Preset props—objects placed onstage in specific locations to be used by actors;
3. Rehearsal props—a stand-in prop used in early rehearsals (e.g., a paper cup for a wine glass);
4. Set props—objects that are a part of the stage setting (for example, furniture, decorations);
5. Wet props—objects that must be replaced each performance (for example, food, beverages, broken or destroyed items).

Public domain. The production status of an older play no longer under royalty restriction. These plays now belong to the community at large and are no longer protected by copyright.

Readers' theatre. A stylized production, often using one or more narrators. Scripts are prominently displayed by all performers, even if dialogue is memorized. Emphasis is on the spoken word rather than on the technical elements.

Rendering. A scaled, color painting of a stage setting from a frontal perspective and usually indicating lighting patterns.

Royalty. A fee paid by the producing organization to the controlling organization for the performance rights to a musical.

Run of the show. The number of performances scheduled; may also include invitational dress rehearsals.

Scenery-shifting rehearsal. A rehearsal emphasizing quick and efficient changes of scenery and involving only the director, technical director, stage manager, and those individuals responsible for moving the scenery.

Sides. The dialogue, song lyrics, and cues of one character bound into a single volume.

Special effects. Lighting, sound, or scenic devices used to produce visual or aural illusions, often of a fantastic nature.

Technical rehearsal. A rehearsal emphasizing one or more technical elements of a production (for example, scenery shifting, light and sound cues, costume and makeup changes, and possible special effects).

Traveler. Any curtain that can be drawn across the stage opening.

Unit set. A single, neutral setting (often involving platforms, ramps, and stairs) to which scenic details and light patterns can be added, or from which they can be deleted, to suggest particular locations.

Wings. Side areas immediately off the onstage playing areas that are used by actors awaiting entrances, and for storage of scenery and properties.

A SELECTED BIBLIOGRAPHY FOR MUSICAL PRODUCERS AND DIRECTORS

Albright, H. D. *Working Up a Part.* Boston: Houghton Mifflin Company, 1962.

Balk, Wesley. *The Complete Actor-Singer.* Minneapolis: University of Minnesota Press, 1977.

Barton, Lucy. *Historic Costume for the Stage.* Boston: Walter H. Baker Company, 1961.

Blunt, Terry. *Stage Dialects.* New York: Intext Publishers, 1967.

Bordman, Gerald. *American Musical Theatre: A Chronicle.* New York: Oxford University Press, 1978.

Coger, Leslie Irene, and White, Melvin R. *Readers Theatre Handbook.* Glenview, Ill.: Scott, Foresman and Company, 1982.

Collier, Gaylan Jane. *Assignments in Acting.* New York: Harper and Row, 1970.

Corson, Richard. *Fashions in Hair.* London: Peter Owen, 1965.

_____. *Stage Makeup.* New York: Appleton-Century-Crofts, 1975.

Crosscup, Richard. *Children and Dramatics.* New York: Charles Scribner's Sons, 1966.

Duffy, Natalie Willman. *Modern Dance: An Adult Beginner's Guide.* Englewood Cliffs, N.J.: Prentice-Hall, 1982.

Egri, Lajos. *The Art of Dramatic Writing.* New York: Simon and Schuster, 1965.

Engel, Lehman. *The American Musical Theatre.* New York: The Macmillan Press Publishing Company, 1975.

_____. *Getting the Show On: The Complete Guidebook for Producing a Musical in Your Theatre.* New York: Schirmer Books, 1983.

Frankel, Aaron. *Writing the Broadway Musical.* New York: Drama Book Specialists, 1977.

Grenbanier, Bernard. *Playwriting.* New York: Thomas Y. Crowell Company, 1961.

King, Nancy. *Theatre Movement.* New York: Drama Book Specialists, 1971.

Kislan, Richard. *The Musical.* Englewood Cliffs, N.J.: Prentice-Hall, Inc., 1976.

Kuritz, Paul. *Playing.* Englewood Cliffs, N.J.: Prentice-Hall, Inc., 1982.

McCaslin, Nellie. *Children and Drama.* New York: David McKay, 1975.

Marshall, Madeleine. *The Singer's Manual of English Diction.* New York: Schirmer Books, 1953.

Mates, Julian. *The American Musical Stage before 1800.* Princeton, N.J.: Rutgers Press, 1962.

Mielzner, Jo. *Designing for the Theatre*. New York: Bramwell House, 1965.

Package Publicity Service, Inc. *Simon's Directory*. 1501 Broadway, Room 1314, New York, New York 10036 (212) 354-1480.

Parker, W. Owen, and Smith, Harvey K. *Scene Design and Stage Lighting*. New York: Holt, Rinehart and Winston, 1975.

Richards, Stanley. *Great Musicals of the American Theatre*. Vol. 2. Radnor, Pa.: Chilton Book Company, 1976.

_____. *Great Rock Musicals*. New York: Stein and Day, Publishers, 1979.

_____. *Ten Great Musicals of the American Theatre*. Radnor, Pa.: Chilton Book Company, 1973.

Robertson, Warren. *Free to Act*. New York: G. P. Putnam's Sons, 1977.

Rodgers, Richard, and Hammerstein, Oscar. *Six Plays by Rodgers and Hammerstein*. New York: Random House, 1963.

Theatre Crafts. Holmes, Pa.: Theatre Crafts Associates, 1977-.

INDEX

About the Authors

Haller Laughlin is Associate Professor of Theatre at the Florida School of the Arts. A much-sought-after director of stock, dinner, and resident theatre musicals, he is the author of *So You Want to Be a Professional Actor?*, co-author of a children's Christmas musical, *Melissa and the Magic Nutcracker*, and an elected member to the Society of Stage Directors and Choreographers.

Randy Wheeler is Associate Professor and Director of Theatre at Valdosta State College in Georgia. A true *homme du théâtre*, he has performed in a variety of roles on stage and in all capacities off stage in college, community, and professional theatre. He is compiling a dictionary of American theatre personnel of the pre–Civil War era.

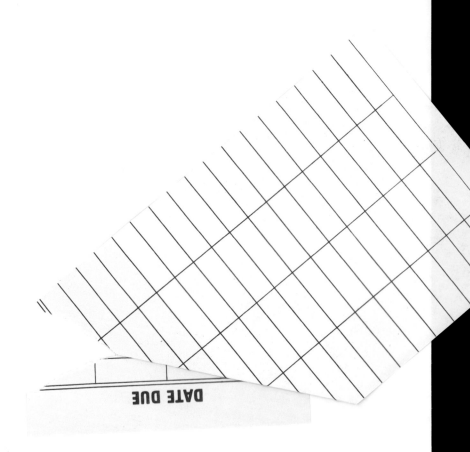

DATE DUE

DEMCO 38-297